RULING YOUR
WORLD

ALSO BY SAKYONG MIPHAM

Turning the Mind into an Ally

RULING YOUR WORLD

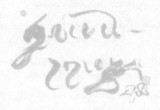

Sakyong Mipham

MORGAN ROAD BOOKS

New York

MORGAN ROAD BOOKS

PUBLISHED BY MORGAN ROAD BOOKS

Copyright © 2005 by Mipham J. Mukpo.

All Rights Reserved

A hardcover edition of this book was originally published in 2005 by
Morgan Road Books.

Published in the United States by Morgan Road Books, an imprint of
The Doubleday Broadway Publishing Group, a division of Random House, Inc.,
New York.
www.morganroadbooks.com

MORGAN ROAD BOOKS and the M colophon are trademarks of
Random House, Inc.

The author and publisher gratefully acknowledge the following for the right to
reprint material in this book:

Chapter 11 originally appeared in a slightly different
version in *Shambhala Sun*.

Traditional verses on page 196 courtesy of the
Nalanda Translation Committee. Used by permission.

Book design by Caroline Cunningham

Library of Congress Cataloging-in-Publication Data
Sakyong Mipham Rinpoche, 1962–
Ruling your world : ancient strategies for modern life / Sakyong Mipham.
p. cm.
1. Religious life—Buddhism. I. Title.

BQ5395.S23 2005
294.3'444—dc22
2005047888

ISBN-13: 978-0-7679-2080-3
ISBN-10: 0-7679-2080-5

PRINTED IN THE UNITED STATES OF AMERICA

3 5 7 9 10 8 6 4 2

To my father,

the first Sakyong,

and

to my teachers,

His Holiness Dilgo Khyentse Rinpoche

and

His Holiness Drupwang Pema Norbu Rinpoche,

for empowering the Sakyong lineage

Contents

Introduction   I

I. THE SECRET OF RULERSHIP

1. *What about Me?*   9

2. *Windhorse*   20

3. *The Ten Percent Advantage*   28

II. THE PATH OF THE TIGER

4. *How to Make a Decision*   41

5. *Understanding Karma*   50

6. *The Utility of Regret*   59

7. *The Virtue of Exertion*   66

8. *Hanging Out with the Right Crowd*   72

9. *The Confidence of Contentment*   79

III. THE PATH OF THE LION

10. *The Virtue of Discipline*   87

11. *No Blame*   93

12. *Letting Love Flow*   100

13. *Generating Compassion*   106

14. *The Confidence of Delight in Helping Others*   111

IV. THE PATH OF THE GARUDA

15. *The Truth about Existence*   121

16. *The Virtue of Letting Go*   128

17. *The Confidence of Equanimity*   133

V. THE PATH OF THE DRAGON

18. *The Virtue of Knowing Selflessness*   143

19. *The Confidence of Wisdom*   152

20. *Attracting Auspiciousness*   158

VI. The Confidence of Rulership

21. *Ruling from the Ground Up*   167

22. *Ruling with Wisdom*   172

23. *Ruling with Power*   178

24. *Ruling Your World*   189

Appendix A: The Posture of Meditation   197

Appendix B: Guidelines for Breathing
  Meditation   198

Appendix C: Guidelines for Contemplative
  Meditation   200

Resources   202

Glossary   207

Acknowledgments   209

Introduction

*Bringing heaven down to earth, into our daily life,
is how we rule our world.*

RECENTLY I VISITED my friends Adam and Allie, the parents of two-year-old Javin. I asked them how parenthood was going, and they replied that what impressed them most was that Javin seemed to know things naturally. They said, "We didn't teach him—nobody did. It's got to have come from somewhere." As human beings, we are so wise. Our minds are vast and profound. In the teachings on rulership, this innate wisdom is known as "basic goodness." It is the natural, clear, uncluttered state of our being. We are all appointed with heaven—great openness and brilliance. Bringing this heaven down to earth, into our daily life, is how we rule our world.

Dawa Sangpo, the first king of the ancient Himalayan

kingdom of Shambhala, once supplicated the Buddha for spiritual guidance. He said, "I'm a king. I have a palace, a family, ministers, subjects, an army, and a treasury. I want to realize enlightenment, but I cannot abandon my responsibilities to pursue spiritual practice in a monastery. Please teach me how to use life in the world to become enlightened."

The Buddha assured the king that he would not have to become an ascetic or a monk in order to attain enlightenment. Indeed, he could practice a spiritual path while fulfilling his many responsibilities. He could become a *sakyong*—a ruler who rules by balancing heaven and earth. Heaven is wisdom. Earth is nitty-gritty experience. When we begin to mix wisdom into our secular life, we have success—both spiritual and worldly. The Buddha said to the king, "Don't be biased. Look at the land and look at your people. If you can develop certainty in the indestructible basic goodness that lies at the heart of everything, then you can rule your world. But becoming a sakyong is a challenging path, since life in the world is full of decisions to make, as well as endless distractions." Taking these instructions to heart, King Dawa Sangpo developed certainty in the view of basic goodness. This vision transformed his kingdom, for it brought inspiration and meaning to people's lives.

My father, the Vidyadhara Chögyam Trungpa Rinpoche—who was born a monk and died a sakyong—led three hundred people out of Tibet in 1959, with the Chinese Communists on their heels. They climbed mountain after mountain, often through deep snow and bitter cold. They ran out of food, so they boiled and ate their yak-skin bags. Some people in the group died; some were captured by the Chinese. They lost many of their possessions, including a thousand-page manuscript on the Shambhala teachings that Rinpoche had written, which was swallowed by a river. According to my mother, in spite of the suffering, they were always cheerful. Finally they crossed the border into India. After enduring many more hardships, Rinpoche eventually came to the West, where he introduced these teachings.

In raising me, my father applied the traditional guidelines that the Buddha had established in his instructions to Dawa Sangpo, continuing the Shambhala lineage of the bodhisattva-warrior and the enlightened ruler. This is a lineage of fearlessness: we are not afraid of our own power to unite heaven and earth. Certain teachings are made for certain times. The Shambhala teachings have appeared in the West at this particular time to pacify aggression, which obstructs our ability to love and care for one another. Aggression produces fear. Fear produces cowardice; we are afraid even of our own thoughts and are therefore ruled by them. The teachings of Shambhala tell us how to establish peace and confidence. In the potential to discover basic goodness and to bring forth wisdom and compassion in our daily life, we all have what we need to become a sakyong—a Tibetan word that means "earth-protector." What we are protecting is the earth of our innate sanity.

If ruling our world stems from developing certainty in our sanity, how do we discover it? The Shambhala teachings instruct us to "put our mind of fearfulness in the cradle of loving-kindness." The most loving environment we can create is on the meditation seat. My father taught me to meditate when I was a child. At the beginning, this meant simply taking time out of my day to reflect on my feelings. Then I learned to stabilize my mind by placing it on the breath. When I had accomplished the precision of this technique, he told me to contemplate impermanence, suffering, karma, selflessness, and compassion. When I was about twelve, he instructed me to meditate and contemplate for one hour a day. He later increased the sessions to two hours. At times I meditated for several days, and eventually for weeks and even months. Since meditation was to be the mainstay of my future vocation, I had the time to do it this way.

When I was a teenager, I explained to my father that I wanted to go camping alone in the wilderness. After pondering it for a few days, he said that this would be a good time. As a parent, he was proud that I wanted to explore the world on my own, and he was concerned about my safety. He wanted to make sure I could carry a heavy backpack, so after loading me up, he had me run up and down the stairs a few times. Having satisfied his concerns, off I went, feeling exuberant.

I hiked for about a week, rarely seeing anyone and encountering all kinds of foul weather—wind, rain, hail. I felt surprisingly happy. Having grown up in situations where there were many people around, I had always been tutored, fed, and served. Feeling alone helped me appreciate what others had done for me, and I also began to discover my own strength as a Shambhala warrior on my way to becoming a ruler. Nature was an excellent teacher, never giving an inch. If I wanted to eat, I had to make a meal; if I wanted to sleep, I had to think ahead and find an appropriate camping spot.

Upon my return, people were relieved, excited, and proud. Although it had been a short trip, I had grown tremendously. Through all the dramatic weather and other challenges, I was left sitting with my mind. I had discovered my own confidence, which gave me confidence in my basic goodness.

My father also trained me in poetry and calligraphy, following the traditional guidelines for educating a future ruler. One day as we were leaning on a railing at our house in Colorado, looking out at a meadow and some pine trees, a hummingbird appeared. It fluttered in several directions and darted off. My father turned to me and said, "Today I will teach you how to write poetry." I have continued to practice and enjoy this art, as well as calligraphy. Such deepening arts teach us to express the inexpressible—love, impermanence, and beauty. Diving into our own profundity, bringing the precision of meditation into physical form, we discover the profundity of life.

In addition, my father made sure that I trained in martial arts—the physical discipline of moving meditation that helps us become less insulated within our own mind. Practicing sports or martial arts gives us natural confidence. We develop a bond of kinship and appreciation with friends.

Breathing fresh air and learning to synchronize mind and body help us develop a healthy sense of self, which allows us to further increase our confidence. We can then offer our understanding to others. I learned Japanese archery—*kyudo*. Initially, we were not allowed even to hold the bow and arrow. Then for the first year of practice, we shot at a target only six feet away, the idea being that if we could develop proper form, hitting the target would not be an issue. Eventually, we shot at a target seventy-five feet away.

Raising a ruler differs from the conventional approach to education, which considers the mind an empty box waiting to be filled. My father once told one of my tutors that in raising a future sakyong or sakyong *wangmo*—earth-protector king or queen—we are educating the sky. The sky perceives, understands, and encompasses everything. There are no boundaries—only possibilities. Educating ourselves as sakyong is therefore not a laborious undertaking. It is filled with appreciation, curiosity, and delight. We are cultivating certainty in basic goodness and developing our noble qualities. When we are connected with basic goodness, it inspires our every breath, action, and thought. With the resulting brilliance and confidence, we can accomplish whatever we wish. This is how we rule our world.

I

The Secret

of Rulership

1

What about Me?

We already have what we need—the opportunity
to weave the tapestry of happiness every day with
the needle and thread of our own mind.

A S A CHILD, I was struck by the story of the prince and
the pauper. The Tibetan version of this story has it that
the prince and the pauper are the same person. Through a series of mishaps, the prince grows up as a pauper, only later to
discover that he is a child of the royal family and the future
ruler of his kingdom. He was always a prince; he was never a
pauper; the only thing that changed was his view. We are in
a similar situation. We are all of royal birth.

In the legend of Shambhala, there is a family of beings
called the Rigdens, who have never strayed from basic goodness, a pure radiance that has never been stained by ignorance, anger, jealousy, or pride. The Rigdens are not some

celestial entities; they represent the ultimate ruler within us all. Tibetan paintings of the kingdom of Shambhala show the Rigdens conquering the negativity of the dark age. They are often depicted sitting on thrones of diamonds, indicating unshakable possession of the awareness of basic goodness, our primordial nature, which is also known as the Great Eastern Sun.

The Rigden king manifests wrathfully, but his armor is always gold, an expression of compassion. His sword represents the incisive wisdom that sees basic goodness. There are pennants on his helmet, which symbolize the courage it takes to bring windhorse—long life, good health, success, and happiness—to others. After the victory of the Rigdens, the story goes, the age of enlightenment arises. The Great Eastern Sun appears on the horizon.

Whether we take this story as literal or metaphorical, the meaning is the same. We all have the potential to be enlightened rulers. The Buddha is an example of a human being who developed this potential. By sitting still and working with his mind, he uncovered essential truths and developed techniques to help the rest of us discover our ability to rule. Since I'm a Buddhist, he is my role model, but obviously basic goodness is not confined to any one tradition. It is the essence of everyone and everything.

We all belong to the family of the Rigdens. Basic goodness, the shimmering brilliance of our being, is as clear as a mountain lake. But we're not certain about our own goodness. We begin to stray from it as soon as we wake up in the morning, because our mind is unstable and bewildered. Our thoughts drag us around by a ring in our nose, as if we were cows in the Indian market. This is how we lose control of our lives. We don't understand that the origin of happiness is right here in our mind. We might experience happiness at times, but we're not sure how we got it, how to get it again, or how long it's going to last when it comes. We live life in an anxious, haphazard state, always looking for happiness to arrive.

When we are confused about the source of happiness, we start to blame the world for our dissatisfaction, expecting it to make us happy. Then we act in ways that bring more confusion and chaos into our life. When our mind is busy and discursive, thinking uncontrollably, we are engaging in a bad habit. We are stirring up the mud of jealousy, anger, and pride. Then the mind has no choice but to become familiar with the language of negativity and develop it further.

When desire or anger takes our mind and says, "You're coming with me," we become paupers. The pauper wakes up each morning with the thought "What about me? Will I get what I want today?" This meditation resonates through our day like a heartbeat. We think, "Will this food make me happy?" "Will this movie make me happy?" "Will this person make me happy?" "Will this new sweater make me happy?" "What about me?" becomes the motivating force of our activity.

Occasionally when I meet with meditation students, their questions show that they are approaching even spiritual practice as a way to make themselves happy. Is my yoga, my tai chi, my meditation making "me" feel better? They are simply using a new guise to perpetuate the old habit of putting themselves first.

This self-infatuated approach is like using unclean fuel. When our motivation is to make "me" happy, the engines of our life run rough. Our self-obsession makes us stressed and ill. The magnet of "What about me?" draws away windhorse—our ability to bring about success—and our mind becomes very small. We lose touch with earth—our potential to give our life meaning—so there's no place for true happiness to land.

In Tibet, trying to achieve happiness without understanding the cause of happiness is called *lotok*, "backward." It's like looking through the wrong end of the binoculars—happiness doesn't get bigger and closer, it gets smaller and farther away. What makes the mind of "me" so small is confused emotion, in Sanskrit, *klesha*—anger, desire, ignorance, and pride. These are obscurations that block our view of basic goodness. They are all very familiar and friendly to us. For many of us, they are simply the tools by which we engage in life. We may think that they're the only tools we have—that pushing hard and clinging tight is the secret to success. This confusion doesn't always show up as a temper tantrum. It also manifests as insidious discursiveness—going over things again and again in our mind, or jumping from one thought to another with "What about me?" playing in the background.

samsara

Being fooled into trying to make things work out for "me" is called *samsara*. This is a Sanskrit word that describes an endless dark age in which we are completely distracted by the agitation that comes from trying to make "me" happy. Our mind is constantly volleying between irritation and desire, jealousy and pride. We are unhappy with who we are, and we are trying to destroy our own suffering, which reflects our basic discontent. As we indulge in this negativity, our mind becomes thick with contamination. This contamination manifests as stress—lack of peace. It is fueled by fear—fear of not knowing what will happen to "me." With the ambition to get what we want and to avoid what we don't, our mind becomes very speedy. We act in ways that hurt others and ourselves. Bewilderment rules our days and nights. We keep imagining that a love affair, a new job, a thinner body, or a vacation is going to lead to happiness. When we get what we want, we feel good, and we become attached. Then the situation changes, and we feel angry. Or somebody else's relationship, job, or body looks better than ours, and we feel jealous.

When we're fooled by the world of appearances, we aren't seeing beyond the surface. Our changing mind keeps us trapped in suffering, the nitpicky details. We lose our desire for deepening and begin to consider the smallest, most irrelevant things important. We'd rather hear a piece of gossip about a celebrity we'll never meet than contemplate the truth. We are more interested in listening to a new song on the radio than in hearing instruction about how to bring meaning to our life. If somebody tries to give us advice, we lash out. Slowing down and relating to life through a discipline like meditation seems like a frivolous luxury.

With this small-mindedness, we have little inspiration to improve our situation in a lasting way, because we don't trust what we can't see—like wisdom and compassion. We have no relationship with the unchanging ground of basic goodness. We want to keep our options open. We think that freedom to keep changing our mind will bring happiness. In fact, the mind that is always changing can only lead to pain.

When we're on the "me" plan, what others say about us has great power. A friend tells us we look good—our mind soars. A colleague tells us we're not pulling our weight at work—our mind sinks. We are like children, one minute laughing and the next minute crying. In reality, praise and criticism are like echoes—they have no substance, no duration. But when we chase our projections like a dog going after a stick, even words have the power to destabilize our mind. We think about what somebody said, over and over. We let it ruin our day.

When we're fooled by the view of "me," our attitude toward wealth is that it's all out there—and we want some. We're like monkeys grabbing at shiny objects. We accumulate so many things that we have no room to appreciate them. Our wanting creates the habit of perpetual hunger and mindless activity. We look at people with the attitude of taking, not of giving. We'll help someone who's becoming powerful and wealthy—somebody who's on the way up. If somebody's slipping, we start to pull away. We don't think twice about fighting with our family or community. We believe that the only way to improve our situation is to keep trying to get a little more for ourselves. We're confused, because we don't understand that we already have what we need—the opportunity to weave the tapestry of happiness every day with the needle and thread of our own mind.

Sometimes we think that power will make us happy. We can't rule our mind, so we try to saddle others with the heavy yoke of our aggression. Far from accomplishing the benefit of others, we can't bear it when something nice happens to them. The word for jealousy in Tibetan means "crowded shoulders." There's room for only one head on our shoulders. We can handle only one person getting things, and that's us. We take some kind of odd thrill in getting mad when the train is late or the power goes out. We're so engrossed in "me" that we forget that others are also suffering.

Crowded shoulders

Our superficial approach extends even to virtue. We may be kind to people in public, but behind their backs, we say snide things. We're generous when we think we'll get something in return. We may be patient about getting what we want, but when life presents us with something that we don't want, like illness, we have no patience. We exert ourselves at work, but when we're alone, we think we can do whatever we like—nobody is watching.

In fact, it is ourselves who should be most concerned about how we act, because we are most affected by our actions. Once when the golfer Bobby Jones was playing in a big tournament, he inadvertently moved his ball a few inches in the rough. He penalized himself, based on what had happened. When someone pointed out to him that no one else had seen the ball move, he said, "I saw it move, and that's all that matters." When I was going into one of my first meditation retreats, I asked my father, Chögyam Trungpa Rinpoche, for some advice. He said, "How you act when you're alone affects the rest of your life." Even in solitude, the ruler engages in virtue.

Virtue is practical, not moralistic. It consists of cultivating thoughts, words, and actions that will help move us out of the "me" plan. As we change our habits—what we do and don't do—we are changing from the outside in. At the same time, what's on the inside begins to come out. We have more space in our mind, and our view gets bigger. We begin to see our inherent richness, the brilliance that's been hiding behind the clouds of stress and anxiety. The nature of our mind is pure, like the sky. Like space, it has a quality of accommodation. Like water, it is clear, with no obstructions or opinions. This is basic goodness, the indestructible nature of our being.

The mind of the pauper is small because it is rooted in attachment—a death grip on life. Fixating on how we want the world to be and trying to make it stay goes against the natural grain. That tightness and the sense of claustrophobia it creates is "me." Our negativity gives us something to hold on to. We think that if we hold on tight enough, we can manipulate the world to make "me" happy. We've tried being angry and desirous hundreds of times. Has anger ever brought genuine happiness? Has desire ever resulted in long-lasting satisfaction?

Who is it that we are protecting with our anger? Who are we trying to get more for with jealousy and desire? The reason that we can't make "me" happy is that there is really no one behind that door. "Me" is just an idea, a concept, a myth. Essentially, it is attachment to a mirage. We're clinging to a fabrication and generating negative emotions in an attempt to protect it.

The king and queen know that happiness doesn't come from out there; it comes from in here. Getting off the "me" plan is the cause of happiness, and learning to see how "me" works is where it starts. It begins with the practice of meditation—just ten minutes or so every day. By stabilizing the mind we learn to connect with space beyond "me"—heaven. Heaven is the natural spaciousness of our mind before we make it small with self-protection. Once our mind becomes more peaceful, we begin to see how "me" is just thoughts, feelings, and emotions made solid.

In meditation practice, we learn to acknowledge and recognize our thoughts without acting on them. We're no longer quite so fooled by appearances. Our mind becomes more flexible, because we begin to see our own projections. We begin to figure out the currency of life: it is all a display of the mind. No longer do we run after the stick of every outside appearance, like a dog. Rather, like a lion, we begin to look at who is throwing the stick—our mind.

Then we hear, contemplate, and meditate on how the mind works and how the world works. This is how we develop certainty in basic goodness. We realize that we are always hearing, contemplating, and meditating, but on a chaotic flurry of thoughts and emotions. Hearing that our friends are splitting up, we contemplate who did what to whom, developing certainty in blame. Hearing that somebody made a lot of money, we develop certainty in jealousy. Our hearing, contemplating, and meditating are haphazard, and the conclusions that we draw often lead us down the road of negativity.

This shortsighted attitude stifles our inherent energy. That natural energy is compassion—in Tibetan, *nyingje*, "noble heart." In Tibetan paintings, buddhas are often depicted sitting on lotuses, which represent our innate yearning for the happiness of others. This self-arising flower is the core of our being. We need to create space in our mind in order to nurture it. The obsession with "me" suffocates it; the flower can't blossom. When we consider others, we allow the flower to bloom. Thinking of others makes our mind bigger, because it brings us joy.

Caring for others is the basis of worldly success. This is the secret that we don't learn in school. If somebody tells us, we don't believe it. We think it must be some kind of joke. How could thinking about others possibly bring me success? Because it seems too simple, we hesitate. In an attempt to outsmart the system, we stick with the "me" plan.

Windhorse takes us beyond the "me" plan. As we release

that small-mindedness, a natural magnetic energy arises. There is something charismatic about us. It's not just that we look good from the outside; we are radiating from the inside out. We exude success and enthusiasm. Like basic goodness itself, our field of power is pure and uncluttered. We are no longer using hope and fear to manipulate the environment one way or another. Our mind is not burdened by trying to maintain the concept and polarity of "me." Because we have aligned ourselves with basic goodness, the environment begins to reflect our open quality. We effortlessly, as if by magic, attract what we need. With certainty in the energy of basic goodness, we are no longer paupers.

Most of us are a mixture of the prince and the pauper. We don't yet know how to rule our world. We're living in a haze—sometimes helping others, sometimes helping ourselves; sometimes happy, sometimes sad. Without the ability to rule our thoughts, we are seduced or abducted by every whim that walks through the door. Only when we have a plan for bringing meaning to our life will we make true progress. The Shambhala path offers practical strategies for developing compassion, confidence, and courage, with our life in the world as the vehicle. The rare and precious teaching that the Buddha offered King Dawa Sangpo recognizes that we are engaged in the world. We have families and jobs and busy schedules. We can use all of it to nurture wisdom and compassion, developing certainty in basic goodness. Following this path is how we join the family of the Rigden king and queen.

2

Windhorse

When we have windhorse, we are able to accomplish what we want without many obstacles.

F OR MANY YEARS, I had the privilege of studying in
India with His Holiness Dilgo Khyentse Rinpoche,
who was like my grandfather. Khyentse Rinpoche was a great
Tibetan meditation master, a teacher of teachers and
kings—among them, His Holiness the Dalai Lama and the
king of Bhutan. He was an incredibly soft-spoken person
who radiated power in a gentle way. Each day he would sit on
a couch or a bed with his students gathered around. He was
old and big and fat, and he liked to wrap his favorite blankets
around his waist. His presence was warm and genuine. His
stuff always looked better than everybody else's. His prayer
beads, his old Tibetan wooden cup—even his blanket—
shone with goodness. In his presence, the value of the most

ordinary item increased—not simply because he owned it but because it attracted others. His energy infected his environment. In his presence there was a sense of natural wealth and success that had nothing to do with money.

That is the power of *lungta*, windhorse. *Lung* is "wind" and *ta* means "horse." You see the image of windhorse printed on the prayer flags that flutter in the breeze all over Tibet. It is the ability to bring about long life, good health, success, and happiness. When we have windhorse, we are able to accomplish what we want without many obstacles. On its back, windhorse carries a wish-fulfilling jewel. This jewel is the wisdom and compassion that it takes to act not on behalf of ourselves but for all beings. This is where real confidence and competence come from. Once we possess this jewel, our life becomes blessed. Whatever we want happens without difficulty. Just as if we were to jump on the back of a horse and ride across the open country, there is nothing in our way. With windhorse, we are like warriors racing over the vast plains of Tibet, our victory banners fluttering in the wind.

I meet many people in my travels, and I can tell just by how they look or speak that fear and stress are reducing their life-force energy. They are hampered by *drip*—a Tibetan word that describes contamination of ourselves and the environment—the depletion that comes from living on the "me" plan. Drip is the opposite of windhorse. Windhorse thrives on discernment and intelligence. Drip thrives on lack of it. Windhorse is the element that emerges when we engage in virtue. Drip is the element that exudes when we engage in aggression and fixation. We think we have to push to get to where we want to go. Windhorse comes from paying attention to how we conduct our lives. Drip comes from feeling that it doesn't make a difference. Windhorse attracts *drala*—the blessing energy that arises when we overcome our own aggression. Drip attracts obstacles. Windhorse is clean fuel. Drip is a layer of goo, like soot from a coal fire. It feels dark and heavy, like having tar in our lungs from smoking. Windhorse uplifts us. Drip thickens our mind. By cultivating negativity, we are neglecting our potential to discover basic goodness, and the pollutant in our system gains the strength to overpower our wisdom and compassion. There is no drala. Life becomes dark and difficult.

I remember asking my father about the first time that he ever saw a car. He was a teenager living in eastern Tibet, quite a remote area. He said that he could smell the car for days before he saw it. He didn't know what the smell was. It just got stronger and stronger, and finally the car arrived. He said that for days after it left, he could still smell it. That's what drip is like.

Drip "drips" on us. We experience it as a film that covers everything. This film is a reflection of negative psychological leftovers in our environment, the exhaust and pollution of the "me" plan. When our mind is habitually agitated and discursive, drip becomes a veil of normality. As if our eyes are not fully open, we expect things to be a little dark and dirty all the time. In being fooled by the veil, we become imprecise. We believe that it doesn't matter what we say, think, do, or eat, so we ignore our mental and physical environment. Acting on self-interest seems natural, and we engage in activities that reduce our life-force energy. We eat food that weakens our system. We speak words that diminish our integrity. We constantly seek entertainment. We wear clothes that make us feel lazy. Living our life in a nonchalant way, we miss so many opportunities. Things just don't work out; our energy is perennially low. We forget about wisdom and compassion. We forget that every moment of our life is important. If we're not exerting ourselves toward virtue, then most likely we'll be swayed into nonvirtue, and "What about me?" will just become stronger.

Drip takes on its own life as obstacles. Accomplishing what we want becomes more difficult. We miss the bus; we get a parking ticket; we become ill. The most serious obstacle is the idea of "me," which keeps us from seeing our own basic goodness. Out of that doubt comes ignorance, and out of ignorance come negative emotions, which produce more harmful acts, which make the dark age darker. Buddhists consider physical illnesses to be the results of previous negative actions; from that point of view, the disease of "me" is the root of all disease. It's the one that keeps samsara going.

Because our mind is weak, we get mad at these obstacles, which feed off our negative emotions. Becoming aggravated increases the power of the obstacle, like throwing gasoline on a fire. Obstacles have no loyalty. The negative energy that anger attracts goes beyond the person who is angry. Like an accident on the highway, one person's obstacle slows everybody down. Its polluting effect lingers for a long time. When everyone is tied up in knots of self-interest, drip rules, and there's no way to foster harmony. We're always in conflict with the environment. This is how drip drains our windhorse and weakens our life force. It blocks our view of basic goodness.

The environment is a support or a deterrent for whatever we want to do. Everything in our environment—food, clothing, places, the hours we keep, the compassion or jealousy of others—affects us. Certain physical environments can have a negative effect on us. Drip can enter through all of our senses. Some foods taste good, but after eating them we feel tired, not nourished. Some music soothes or relaxes us; other music leaves us feeling disturbed. Some people energize us; others exhaust us. There are certain places we shouldn't go in our mind. Angry, grasping, or greedy thoughts darken our view and deplete our energy.

Just as we should avoid environments that encourage drip, we should gravitate toward environments that attract drala. Drala means "above the enemy." The enemy is whatever weakens windhorse. Drala gathers in people, spaces, and situations that reflect gentleness, discipline, harmony, and appreciation; speed, chaos, and carelessness repel it. As the link between our own vastness and the vastness of the universe, drala is the blessing energy of reality—magic. When we have the courage to cultivate wisdom and compassion, drala connects the power of our being with the power of things as they are, because we are rising above the enemy of negativity.

Drip and drala may sound like superstition. If we take the word *superstition* to mean "conceptual," then yes, drala and drip are concepts, but so is everything else—you, me, and the world of appearances. The great teachers of the past have said that the polluting energy of drip and the blessing energy of drala exist, both in our own mind and in our environment, and that they influence us. Drip contaminates us and makes life difficult. It is the junk that clogs the wheels of the machinery of life. Inviting drala into our life is how we clean it. Windhorse is a sign that the machine is working well.

We all have basic goodness—the energy of windhorse—just waiting to be discovered. We are and always have been complete and perfect beings in a complete and perfect world. If we're feeling depressed, basic goodness doesn't diminish. Its profundity is beyond mood or manipulation. We sometimes hear it knocking on the door of anger or obsession, saying, "You don't have to do this." We can feel it, and we can sometimes experience it, but somehow we lose confidence in it. Then we project solidity onto ourselves and the world, dividing it into "us" and "them."

This ignorance keeps us in the darkness of samsara, which stems from our being fooled at the most fundamental level: we are projecting solidity onto a fluid situation. Instead of seeing the transparency of anger, depression, or hesitation, we identify with confused emotion, which thickens our mind with drip. We fool ourselves into thinking that we have to get something to fix our life or destroy somebody to make it okay, and then we engage in further nonvirtue. We can't see that the battle is happening only in our mind. The teachings of rulership instruct us how to leave this cycle of suffering behind.

The king and queen know that drip comes about through lack of awareness and *payu*—discernment. We are not careful of our environment, and we make decisions haphazardly, without vision. Instead of opening the veil of drip to see our basic goodness, we decide to follow our desire to make "me" happy. We decide to cling to thoughts rather than let them go, and then we decide to turn them into actions that harm ourselves and others. Without really understanding what we're doing, we decide to be angry instead of patient, to be lazy instead of exerting ourselves, to get rather than to give. We decide to seek entertainment instead of engaging in our lives. This backward approach creates stress and imbalance, so obstacles arise, and we can't achieve our wishes, which are always rooted in a deep longing to connect with basic goodness, even though we've forgotten it. No matter how thick the drip, something in us knows that basic goodness is there. That is wisdom trying to peek through.

In Tibet, people go to deeply accomplished masters to help them turn the tide of negativity into something positive. Ultimately, these experienced meditators can't wipe our drip away, but they can help us learn to stabilize our mind and teach us how to make the right decisions so that we can overcome it ourselves. They can give us teachings that help us purify drip, raise windhorse, and attract drala.

Since I was very young, I have studied the art of rulership. Some of these teachings came directly from my father, a descendant of the legendary warrior-king Gesar of Ling. Others came from texts that were carried on horseback and on human back, across rivers and through forests, in order to guarantee their survival. Tibetans are very practical people. They have passed these teachings down because they work. They are rooted in the images of four mythical creatures that represent the kind of confidence that we need in our daily lives to uncover the wish-fulfilling jewel of wisdom and compassion. Cultivating the contentment of the tiger, the delight of the lion, the clear-seeing equanimity of the garuda, and the playful wisdom of the dragon is how we harness windhorse, creating spiritual and worldly success.

In the old days, people would travel great distances to receive teachings such as these. These days, however, the world is in a perilous state, and some of us don't even understand the importance of working with our own mind and environment. I hope that by broadcasting this ancient wisdom, I can inspire many people to cultivate confidence in basic goodness, love toward others, and the courage to bring their vision down to earth. In bringing about our own happiness by blending these teachings into our lives, we can also change the course of our future.

3

The Ten Percent Advantage

The most practical way to ensure forward move-ment on the path of rulership is to train for a short time each day in changing our attitude—just ten percent.

ONE OF MY TEACHERS once said to me, "What is the difference between the Buddha and ourselves? The Buddha has complete confidence in basic goodness. He knows from direct experience that basic goodness is here, whether we have confidence in it or not. We are all awake, loving, brilliantly wise beings. We have the wisdom and com-passion of a universal monarch lying within us like dormant seeds waiting for the sun. We think that we're 180 degrees from enlightenment, but we're only a few degrees off."

I've always found this bit of wisdom and encouragement heartening, because there are days when the qualities of a buddha might as well be in a different galaxy. In fact, our wisdom and compassion are always available. What it takes to see this is not a trip to the Far East or a radical change in lifestyle but a subtle shift in our attitude. Learning to rule is a matter of developing confidence in basic goodness.

To develop this confidence, we must become skillful in gathering virtue every day. Most of us wake up in the morning after not having had quite enough sleep. Feeling a little groggy, we stumble into the bathroom or the kitchen, and then we continue to stumble through our day without much forethought. We're habituated to a self-centered view—one that's coming from always feeling slightly pissed off, depressed, or anxious. Expecting to flip "What about me?" overnight toward becoming contented, joyful, accommodating, and wise may seem as realistic as last night's dream.

If you want to get your body in shape, you don't expect a radical difference after one week of training. Nor do you start by spending five hours a day in the gym. With a little bit of walking, running, lifting, and stretching, you feel more refreshed and inspired by the day—and before you know it, you're stronger, you've got more energy, and you're getting better sleep.

Similarly, the most practical way to ensure forward movement on the path of rulership is to train for a short time each day in changing our attitude—just ten percent. Overdoing it could derail the whole process, like running too far too fast, or lifting more weight than we can bear. That's why in the beginning I encourage people to meditate in ten-minute periods, without the goal of seeing immediate results. The sensible approach is to tell ourselves, "I can still be irritated ninety percent of the time. But with ten percent of my mind and heart, I'll try putting others first."

When I wake up in the morning, first I stabilize my mind by placing it on the breath. When a thought arises, I acknowledge it and return my focus to the breath. Then I orient my mind in the direction of how I can be helpful, how I can learn more that day, or how I can raise my windhorse. I foster compassion and rouse *prajna*—a Sanskrit word that means "best knowledge"—about how I'm going to live my day. By stabilizing my mind on the breath, I'm putting my feet on the ground, like the tiger. By contemplating meaningful thoughts, I'm uplifting my mind with discipline, like the lion. I'm setting my attitude. Life is always trying to dismount us from the saddle of basic goodness. I know that if my mind is in the right place at the beginning, I am going to have the upper hand in ruling my day.

Developing confidence in basic goodness is a twenty-four-hour-a-day practice. In our short formal practice—ten minutes or so every morning—we use the essential neutrality of our mind to let positive forces permeate our being. We are resting in our inherent peace, honing our skills to be a better person, and gathering the strength to live the rest of our day well. We are gaining more insight, removing veil upon veil of hesitation, ignorance, and doubt. (See the appendices for instruction that will help you begin to practice.)

Then we step into our life and apply our contemplation

to our daily activities by engaging in virtue. Connecting with heaven each day, we are able to bring virtue into the earth of our daily world by using relative prajna—knowing how things work and thinking accurately. Having enlarged our mind in meditation, we continue to cultivate thoughts and actions that take us in a positive direction—away from the "me" plan and toward peace, compassion, and wisdom. When the events of the day destabilize our mind, we use mindfulness and awareness to bring it back to our breath or to the topic of our morning contemplation.

As I live my day, I always try to have a contemplation going—whether I'm talking to people, riding in a car, giving teachings, or eating. This can be as simple as bringing my mind back to the thought "May others be happy" at every opportunity. Or I might focus on selflessness or how to help someone who is ill. That power of intention helps me turn confusion on its ear and enjoy my life. When self-absorption arises, I use the precision of my morning meditation to turn the energy inside out. I find that the more I do this, the less worried I feel. Each day is an opportunity to sharpen and deepen the conclusions I've drawn in my morning practice.

People occasionally come to me wanting to abandon their worldly lives in order to pursue meditation full-time. They wonder if this is the "spiritual" thing to do. I tell them that what makes our life spiritual or worldly is not our vocation but our view. If we want a life with meaning, we need to have a plan for connecting causes and conditions so that what we do in the world now will have a positive effect on the future.

This attitude leads to lungta, windhorse—the ability to ride the inherent strength and vitality of our awareness. We begin to use our lives to manifest in a strong way, as opposed to an aggressive way, reviving our love and kindness and expressing it with wisdom.

We're often confused about our purpose in the world, because we mistakenly associate worldly activity with negative emotion. We think that being successful means accomplishing what we want with ambition and greed. Being trapped by negative emotions and perpetuating them is not worldly success—it is worldly ignorance. People often say, "Ignorance is bliss." Actually, ignorance is pain. Knowledge is bliss. Developing certainty in the view of basic goodness and respecting the law of *karma*—causes and conditions—are how to cause happiness.

Karma moves in two directions. If we act virtuously, the seed we plant will result in happiness. If we act nonvirtuously, suffering results. The words *virtue* and *nonvirtue* may sound moralistic, but karma is not based on any kind of judgment. It's just how reality works. If we're at the cosmic bank and we give the teller self-obsession and anger, what we get in exchange is based on the currency of pain. If we give the teller generosity or patience, what we get in return is based on the currency of happiness. The happiness we get in exchange for virtue could happen on the spot, or it could be delayed until sometime in the future.

One Tibetan word for *worldly* means "fearless." This is different from the fearlessness of the ruler, which starts with the

open-mindedness and precision developed through meditation. It describes a world where we have no fear of our confusion. We indulge our anger and greed as means to solve our
problems, without fear of the repercussions. We think that
we can get mad and there won't be any consequences. We're
counting on karma not working, or at least disappearing until we're finished yelling at somebody.

If this state of karmic denial were a place, we'd all own
time-shares there. But it isn't a place, it's a view—"What
about me?" We are fearless in putting ourselves first. We fearlessly get mad, we fearlessly get jealous, we fearlessly feel
proud. "What about me?" is the attitude of paupers and
fools. It's like not being afraid of bacteria. Either we don't
know about infection or we think we're immune to it, so we
don't wash our hands or clean our wounds. We are fearless
because we're ignorant. We're ignoring how karma works.

The only way to loosen the grasp of karma is to engage in
virtue. We don't have to isolate ourselves from the world to
do this; according to the tradition of Shambhala, being in the
world can be the basis of spiritual success. It all depends on
our attitude. Most of the time we are engaged in either virtue
or nonvirtue. We are attracting the blessing energy of drala
and strengthening windhorse—the ability to bring about
success—because we're rising above aggression. Or we're ac-
cumulating drip and inviting obstacles because we're sinking
into the "me" plan.

Playing the game of ten percent means slowing down,
stepping back, and asking, "What is my view? Am I fearless

with wisdom, ready to help others? Or am I fearless with ignorance, ready to indulge in negativity?" Drawing upon the reservoir of experience we had in our morning contemplation will help us remember that we already decided earlier in the day to use compassion. We're not going to change our mind now and solidify a bad mood into anger. By returning to the theme of our contemplation instead of reacting to the ups and downs of life, we are building cloud banks of virtue. Every day we gain a little more insight into the power of the mind—how it creates confusion and how thinking accurately and acting virtuously keep us grounded in our own wisdom.

That ten-minute period of sitting is important. We can stabilize our mind and then contemplate suffering, impermanence, or selflessness. We can contemplate how to lead a good life, or how we can do something meaningful today. We can contemplate what others might need. Perhaps we simply try to kindle a small ember of compassion in our heart and take that into ten percent of our day. Although this warmth might be dwarfed by the raging inferno of the "What about me?" contemplation next door, later in the day, compassion seems to come more naturally, and to make more sense.

We can contemplate laughing at ourselves and try to keep ten percent of our mind open to that for the day, watching the other ninety percent taking everything so seriously. That ninety percent is made up of civil servants who don't want to rock the boat of habit. They're on the government payroll. They just want to sit in their offices and stamp the forms that come through with ME, ME, ME. That ten percent looks at the ninety percent with a smile and says, "You put so much hard work into staying on the 'me' plan, trying to keep everything together—ambition, fame, wealth. How ridiculous! You're going to have to do it all over again tomorrow, and for what? Most of your effort just fortifies worry, frustration, and fear."

That ten percent is the glitter in our mind just off in the corner that says, "Let's try leading life in a slightly different way today." It's the break in the clouds that the sun shines through. With that ten percent of an attitude change, we're beginning to buck the system. That is the genuine ruler— not the one who is stamping ME on everything out of fear of doing anything different. The ten percent who changes our day is the one who thinks every moment of life is special. The ninety percent is the irritated, speedy little "me" who says, "I'm busy. Leave me alone. There's nothing new under the sun." The ten percent is saying, "We are the sun."

How much of our day do we spend holding negative thoughts in our mind? These moods are temporary, but they feel so deep-rooted that we think they are ourselves. In meditating on negative emotions, "me" is the habit that we are ingraining. In becoming so familiar with the habit of "me," we begin to mistake it for the nature of our mind. It does seem to be our basic state, and as a meditation, it seems almost effortless. Our whole life can pass in this fashion. However, the result of placing our mind on these negative emotions and keeping it there is not pleasant. We forget to breathe. By the end of the day, we may feel anxious, depressed, and exhausted. It's even hard to sleep, because we have been ingraining disturbing, negative thoughts and images all day.

The ruler takes advantage of the neutrality of the mind. We decide to decrease the percentage of time spent in negative emotion, and increase the amount of time spent in thoughts and ideas that lead somewhere. If we place our mind on thoughts that are based on compassion and wisdom, that's what the mind will become familiar with, and like any habit, it will increase. We can pour a glass of "What about you?" in our mind instead of a glass of "What about me?" By bringing a bigger mind into our daily activity, we are changing our attitude.

Playing the game of ten percent is all about our attitude. Our attitude is like the flag bearer in a military charge. Everybody follows the flag, because that's where the fight is. When our attitude goes through the mud, that's where all our thoughts will go. When our attitude goes to the top of the mountain, all our thoughts will follow. Changing our attitude is the way to effect change in our life. Just as when we want to give up sugar or caffeine, introducing the change gradually has a snowball effect.

Runners talk about establishing a base—a consistent regimen for building endurance and strength. Once you have a base, even if you stop running, it is easy to pick it up again, because the body has become familiar with running. It knows how to run. In beginning to run, I noticed this myself. Once I built a base, I had confidence. I could look around, see where I was going, and enjoy my surroundings. Before I built a base, I was struggling. I had no space in which to appreciate the day. Similarly, in placing our mind on the breath, we build a base of stability that leads to peace. In contemplating truths about existence, we build a base of knowledge that leads to wisdom. The more we cultivate stability and knowledge, the more clearly we see, and the more confident we feel. Because we have a strong base, we feel like engaging in virtue. We enjoy being generous and patient.

Making a ten percent shift in our attitude every day has monumental consequences. As we venture onto the path of the tiger, lion, garuda, and dragon, practicing each of their virtues becomes a wedge in a crack in the rock of self-absorption. Every time we rest in contentment, every time we help others, every time we see through our attachment, every time we relax into our own wisdom, we are pouring water on that wooden peg. Eventually it is able to crack the conceptuality and fear that keep us trapped in the claustrophobia of "me." Our basic goodness is revealed, and we live our life with meaning.

II

THE PATH
OF THE TIGER

4

How to Make a Decision

Venturing onto the path of the tiger, we place our paws carefully. We respect karma; we know that every decision we make has repercussions.

THE KING AND QUEEN conquer not with aggression or self-interest but with payu—discernment. Payu is the most important tool in life, because being alive involves making one decision after another, knowing what to do and when. If we have not developed a standard for making decisions, we make poor choices based on living life backward—engaging in negative emotions and feeling frustrated that they don't bring satisfaction. How can we break out of the "me" plan if we don't apply discernment? No matter how modern the time, the combination of klesha—negativity—and karma will continue to produce suffering, whether we think about it or not. No technology can alter the mechanics of klesha and karma. In deciding to live according to the principle of causes and conditions, we realize that we don't have the luxury of being cavalier. We can't engage in negative activity, expecting it to turn out well. On the path of the tiger, we begin to look at our lives with an eye to what to cultivate and what to discard.

I've received many instructions from my teachers about how to be a ruler. The simplest and most helpful is "Upon arising, have a positive and open attitude." Before we even get out of bed, we can decide to rest in an open-minded, inquisitive space. After focusing our mind on the breath, we can take out the mirror of payu and say, "What decisions do I have to make today? How will I use them to move forward on the path of virtue?" This is how we bring discernment into our daily activity.

In the Shambhala teachings, discernment is associated with the tiger. The tiger is completely alert, whatever it is doing. It respects its surroundings. It doesn't rush into things. It knows when it must hunt on the plains and when it must go to a cool place and rest. The tiger doesn't run around in circles looking for something to eat. First it sits quietly and surveys the landscape to see what is there; then it pounces with exertion.

The mind of the tiger is humble, free from arrogance. It looks before it leaps, and whatever it is doing, it is completely engaged. This quality of meekness connects it with the earth. Here in the West, we associate meekness with weakness. The Tibetan word for *meek* also means "content." The tiger's contentment comes from knowing that everything it needs is contained in the present moment.

Our mind is always being distracted by thoughts of what already happened and ideas about what could happen, but the only thing that is really happening is what is happening now. In breathing meditation, we cultivate mindfulness and awareness of the present moment by focusing our mind on the breath. We are learning to be where we are by synchronizing body and mind. When we sit correctly, the body can relax and be less of a nuisance to the mind. At the same time, connecting with the mind's natural stability and space invigorates the body, like breathing fresh air. That vitality and confidence is windhorse, which is literally rooted in the wind, our breath. The wind element runs throughout our body, and the mind is carried on this wind. Placing our mind on the breath, noticing when thoughts steal our focus, and coming back to the breath is like finding a really nice place to live; we're satisfied, so we don't go out looking for more. We know we have enough.

Having learned to sit, now we learn to walk. Like the tiger, we connect with the earth mindfully, with awareness of what we are doing. We respect karma; we know that every decision we make has repercussions for the future. We slow down and look at the lay of the land before deciding what to say and not to say, what to do and not to do. For example, if our child is misbehaving, we factor in all the possibilities before we react—"What are my choices?" Then we self-reflect—"What is my attitude?" This allows us to determine the virtuous course—"What shall I cultivate? What shall I discard?"—before we speak or act. This is not paranoia; it is care and awareness. Knowing where we are, moving slowly, and determining our action carefully, we are stabilizing our strategy for bringing meaning to our life.

What derails payu is lack of direction. We're still caught up in the changing mind of "me"; we're not convinced that virtue leads to happiness. Without a strong motivation to use discernment, we buy into our habit of running around in circles of meaningless thought. We forget about the space that lies beneath that agitation. We get caught up in worry, irritation, or laziness, and making decisions becomes a matter of trial and error based on mood, so we end up making the same bad choices over and over again. Our wind is wild; we're too distracted to connect the heaven of our mind with the earth of our activity.

According to many wisdom traditions, these are symptoms of a dark age. "Dark" means that we are nearing the end of a brighter time, as when the sun is setting at the end of the day. The light is waning, and the dregs of negativity are extinguishing our wisdom. Like a bar at closing time, it's dark and dingy, and we are intoxicated with self-infatuation. We forget how to conduct ourselves. In a last-ditch effort to get what we want, we give in to anger and jealousy, aggression and desire.

Over a thousand years ago, Padmasambhava, the great teacher who brought Buddhism from India to Tibet, predicted that this particular dark age would be distinguished by our increasing cleverness. Our discursive minds would run rampant. We would create myriad ways to keep ourselves entertained, becoming experts in how to spend free time. We would use our intellect not for betterment but for hanging out in one form of distraction or another, constantly on holiday. Padmasambhava predicted that as we became more shrewd and clever, compassion would seem increasingly futile, and we would lose the knowledge of how to bring meaning to our lives. Our windhorse would weaken. At the same time, the number of weapons, diseases, and starving people would grow. Our negative emotions would increase as our motivation to lead a meaningful life—a life of virtue—waned. Our physical appearance would deteriorate as we processed this negativity.

It is startling to see the eerie accuracy of these predictions. Over the last hundred years, our increasing cleverness has resulted in technologies that have improved our lives in many ways. At the same time, it has increased our capacity to distract our minds. We are trapped in a belief that acquiring things will make us happy. Fear threatens to color everything we do. Fear produces cowardice; compassion seems less realistic, and anger seems more practical. When we allow discursiveness and negative emotions to run unchecked, we weaken windhorse and produce our own dark age.

In this particular dark age, our distraction often manifests as speed. Speed kills the space in which we could appreciate what we're doing. That frantic quality creates its own power and momentum, which begin to rule us. Because we can't rest in the present moment, we can't be satisfied; we conduct our life aggressively. We employ jealousy, competition, fixation, and irritation to chase after appointments, phone calls, and meetings—whatever it takes to get us where we think we need to go. When our day runs rough, it's because these negative emotions are creating "me" bumps in the road. Like speed bumps, they are telling us to slow down and use payu. But without the meekness of the tiger, we're not able to hear them.

Mastering our life begins with the ability to see how we block the way to our own contentment. In our sitting practice, we're trying to penetrate our speedy exterior by reducing our activities and stabilizing our ability to be present. Then we carry that practice into our day, continually reflecting on what to cultivate and what to discard in order to strengthen windhorse. We realize that wanting to be anywhere but where we are, doing anything but what we're doing, is an unnecessary move that throws us off balance. Using payu is how we bring our balance back. With the discernment of the tiger, we learn to slow down, look at where we are, and appreciate our situation.

The Buddha says, "Let's get things straight. The beings in other realms number the grains of sand in all the deserts and oceans. Human beings number the grains of sand on a fingernail. Animals have minds, but if you tell them that they are going to die tomorrow, they have no way of comprehending it. You're in a good place for developing knowledge." When we contemplate our life, we see that he seems to be right. Being human is a precious situation, and we shouldn't waste time in useless activities. This conclusion motivates us to look at what to cultivate and what to discard. We can decide to let go of unnecessary activity instead of wanting more. We can decide to be focused instead of distracted. We can decide to exert ourselves toward appreciating our life and using it to cultivate virtue, instead of being aggressive about filling it up. Aggression and ambition have only produced speed, and now we're always in a panic.

Watching champion runners and golfers on television, I see this principle at work. They often seem to be moving in slow motion, yet they are running faster than others or hitting the ball farther, with more precision, because they have eliminated unnecessary moves. I noticed this same quality in the presence of my teacher Khyentse Rinpoche. It often seemed as if nothing much was happening—he was sitting on a bed and we were gathered at his feet. Yet at the end of the day he would have composed poems, written essays, and taught us *dharma*— the truth of how things are. His accomplishment was effortless and graceful, because it was fueled by discernment and exertion.

Payu is the first step in taking charge of our life. It is like a mirror that shows us what to accept and what to reject. What to accept is whatever liberates us from the "me" plan, and what to reject is what keeps us bound to it. Often when we arise in the morning, we are totally confused about this. From the moment we wake up, we put ourselves first. We can go through the whole day feeling like the world is out to get us. Payu looks at this attitude and asks, "Who decided to make me feel this way?" Our mind is the king and queen, so we are always following our own command. At any moment, we can slow down, look around, and remember that we're in a precious situation called the human realm. Our capacity to self-reflect gives us the power to take control of our mind.

We'd often rather put our mind on the treadmill of discursiveness and entertainment than relax. Then we wonder, "Why is nothing turning out the way I want?" Tiger mind creates a little gap in which we can look at our choices. We could get mad or not get mad. We could manipulate or not manipulate. We could become desirous and fixate. We could get jealous or not. It's up to us. Wisdom and compassion begin with cultivating discernment—not just reacting to what happens.

Using payu throughout the day is not about being our own police; it's about using our life to encourage virtue. On the path of rulership, there's no one standing over us, telling us we'll go to hell if we don't do the right thing. By meditating and contemplating, we learn to see firsthand that when we relate to our life in a shortsighted way, running on the fumes of hope and fear that arise from self-absorption, we send ourselves straight to the land of anxiety, suffering, and misfortune.

Deep inside, most of us know what we should or shouldn't be doing. Continuously fighting with spouses or co-workers is a signal that everyone is engaging in nonvirtue. With payu, we see that we can be small-minded and jump into the fray, or we can be preemptive, enlisting a bigger mind—even if that means walking away. We have the power to determine what we will and will not do. If we have eaten too much, gone on a shopping spree, gotten into an argument, we can reflect upon whether it is virtue or nonvirtue. We can ask, "What is the result of my action? Do I feel imprisoned or liberated? Am I content? Do I have regret?"

At the end of the day, before we go to sleep, we can open our mind again, take out the mirror of payu, and ask, "How did I handle myself today?" This moment of self-reflection shows us where we encouraged virtue and where we went against the grain. Life was telling us one thing—accept, let go, be kind—and sometimes we couldn't be that big. We yelled at somebody, we tried to manipulate, we were so fixated that we couldn't be generous. With payu, we assess what happened and use the past to determine what we want to do in the future. We become students of cause and effect.

With payu, we are using decision making as a way to stabilize our mind and strengthen our windhorse. We become more efficient about how we spend our time. We cut out unnecessary moves. We are no longer living life on a commission basis, because we have a compass that is pointing us in the direction of a meaningful life. We begin to see that making decisions with others in mind—even returning a phone call when we don't feel like it—is how we get out of the "me" plan.

Having made a decision with payu, the tiger sticks with it; it doesn't look back. Changing our decision sets up a bad habit. It reinforces decision making as an expression of bewilderment and ignorance, instead of as a path toward wisdom and freedom. Lack of certainty then thickens our consciousness, drip sets in, and making decisions becomes even harder.

Generally, whatever we do—whether it is good or bad—will only increase if we keep doing it. That is the nature of the mind. Repeating habits only strengthens them. The tiger relies on this truth. Payu encourages us to repeat good habits and conduct in order to make those patterns stronger. With payu, we will be able to change bad habits for the better. Without payu, those bad habits will never change. Little mind becomes smaller with bad habits. Big mind becomes bigger with good ones.

5

Understanding Karma

With appreciation, discernment, and exertion—
the tools of the tiger—not only can we rule our
life now but we can also rule our future.

THE TIGER IS DISCERNING because it understands
the law of karma. *Karma* is a Sanskrit word that means
"action." It describes the continuity of occurrences that
weaves the fabric of life. It is not a linear dynamic in which
one thing happens and therefore another thing happens.
Many causes and conditions come together for one thing to
occur. That one thing then joins the next set of causes and
conditions that coalesce for something else to occur. In any
one moment, there is both cause and effect. Every cause is an
effect, and each effect is also a cause.

Karma is a worldly truth that anyone can see—the
process of things coming together and having a particular

repercussion. For example, the moon shines on a lake, causing a reflection. Or sunlight hits a magnifying glass, creating fire. We see someone else eating ice cream, and suddenly we want ice cream, too. Events occur, and as a result, a third event takes place. The moon's reflection doesn't exist independently but, like magic, arises from a gathering of causes and conditions.

Like gravity, karma is so basic that we often don't even notice it. But karma is happening everywhere. Whatever we see is a meeting of interdependent causes and conditions—not a snapshot but a moving picture. If we walk down the street, we are dependent on the ground being there, on having good health, on having a mind that can make our body move, and on having the time to walk and a place to walk to. Those are all dependently related. In Buddhism we talk about karma in terms of how it lays the ground for us to move from lifetime to lifetime. Even if we don't believe in lifetimes, we can look at karma as how we move from past to present to future.

Karma sometimes manifests very directly. We eat a meal and we feel full. We turn the key and the car starts. A more subtle interconnectedness has to do with our thoughts, actions, and words. One word too many, and our friend blows his lid. Two little words, and we've married somebody. We never know at exactly what moment one action or word is going to trigger another, but everything we do sets something else in motion. This is why the tiger places its paws carefully.

Whether or not we think about the law of karma—

whether or not we even know it exists—it is always in effect. It governs every corner of our being. Karma cannot be deceived. It keeps unfolding. It is painfully democratic. Whether we are rulers or subjects, drivers or pedestrians, teachers or students makes no difference. We cannot opt out of it. There is no time out in life. Whatever we do lays a seed in our deepest consciousness, and one day that seed will grow. Every thought that occurs, especially if we water it with intention, plants a seed. The karmic seed we plant might rest in the depth of our mindstream for ten billion lifetimes waiting for the necessary conditions to occur, but once they do, it will ripen. If I'm feeling really upset, thinking, "I am going to do something about this," I am planting the seed of a rebirth into the realm of irritation. As long as I water that seed, I am creating an environment in which it is harder for seeds of love to grow. By the same token, if I water seeds of love, anger will have fewer opportunities to ripen.

Our seed ripens not for another person but only for ourselves. We make karma whether or not someone else knows what we did. It may not make the front page, but that doesn't mean it didn't happen. Whatever we are doing right now, the result will definitely appear. The tiger looks at the actions of body, speech, and mind, and asks, "What is my intention?" "Which seeds am I nurturing?"

Buddhist teachings about karma often use the example of how a seed becomes a fruit. The seed is the main cause. Seven stages describe how the plant develops on the outer level: the seed, the sprout, the leaf or sapling, the trunk, the

branch, the flower, and then the fruit. What is the cause of
the sprout? It is the seed. What is the cause of the trunk? It
is the sapling. How does it grow? It utilizes water, soil, and
sunlight. These are the causes and conditions that bring the
fruit into being. This is very basic. Everybody knows how a
garden grows. But once we begin to talk about the mind, it
quickly gets complicated.

When we are caught in the force and speed of previous
actions running through our life, we re-create the root ignorance from which confusion arises: our basic goodness is ob-
scured by the illusion of duality. The moment we have split
the world into self and other, we are caught in the wind of
samsara, the cycle of suffering. We are like a magician who
casts a spell and begins to believe in it, then can't find his way
out. Without even thinking about how things really are, we
walk around with a sense of permanence. Conditions all
around us change, but we stubbornly maintain our sense that
"me" is real and solid.

The ignorance that believes itself to be "me" has impulses—virtuous, nonvirtuous, and neutral—that lead to
actions. These confused actions condition our consciousness in the next moment and, according to the teachings of
Buddhism, in the next lifetime. "Me" is made of forms, feelings, perceptions, impulses, and consciousness. These are
the elements that we congeal into an imaginary self. Our
senses make contact with the world around us, and we crave
pleasant experiences, avoid unpleasant ones, and ignore the
rest. This craving leads to appropriating—fixation on these

experiences—and we have given birth to karmic results for the next moment—or lifetime—which in turn age and die.

Even though understanding karma begins by trying to understand ignorance, these links of dependent arising are all happening all the time. Thinking of them as a linear sequence doesn't work. That is why we say that they are dependently related. Ignorance is not necessarily first, even though it is always present. In order for ignorance to happen, lots of other causes have already occurred.

Physics and Buddhism come close together at this point. They both say that the world is not stagnant, even perceptually. Buddhism teaches that consciousness, as well as forms and phenomena, is arising over and over again, 360 times in the snap of a finger. Physics tells us that even though the world looks solid, it's actually an arrangement of constantly moving atomic and subatomic particles. The world is an interplay of movement. Contact with phenomena is the point at which we isolate and freeze that movement. Our sense perceptions can't deal with the chaos. It is so bewildering that consciousness freeze-frames our experience and says, "That's an apple." "That's a piece of chocolate cake." This happens very early in our development. Klesha arises when we say, "I want that piece of cake, and I'll do anything to get it."

If we take the Buddha's word for it, we've been creating actions based on this confusion for many lifetimes. Therefore we have no idea what seeds we are watering. When actions are imprinted in our deepest consciousness, they do not go away on their own. Their potency will continue, unless we do something about it. Our whole life is riddled with causes and conditions that are producing all kinds of results. Karmic events may seem illogical, but that's because we don't understand all the causes and conditions. In Tibet we say, "Only a buddha can explain the reason for every color in a peacock's feathers." Only someone who has fully developed his or her wisdom can truly understand all the causes and conditions and the interdependence that is taking place.

We may not be able to do much about previous actions, but we have the opportunity to change the course of future karma by what we do in the present. That is why on the path of the tiger we use discernment to cultivate virtue and discard nonvirtue. We are not simply trying to be good, we are basing our activity on our observation of how things actually work. If we're using nonvirtue as fuel for living, we're going to feel all the bumps on the road. We become our own enemy, because the karma of a nonvirtuous act is that more negativity comes along. If we don't take care of our body, we get sick. If we aren't careful in our speech, we harm ourselves and others. Engaging in gossip means that people will gossip about us. If we lie, the result will be that others deceive us. The result of getting angry is that people will be more hostile toward us in the future; we'll only experience more irritation. The result of greed is that we'll just want more. Pride in our view makes it hard to hear the truth. The result of all nonvirtuous action is that we become more defensive, more entrenched in "me." We are trading the wish-fulfilling jewel for a rock. Eventually that rock weighs windhorse down. After a while we feel that there's nothing to live for. That funky feeling is drip. It means that drala has deserted us.

We may think we've acquired some happiness by engaging in negativity. Perhaps we think that our ambition has brought us a beautiful house, a nice car, a loving family, and all the money we want. But according to the law of karma, that happiness came from previous virtuous actions. Buddhists say that it could have come from something we did in a previous lifetime. Even if we don't believe in past lives, if we think nonvirtue produces happiness, all we have to do is look at those people who have seemingly achieved some happiness by indulging in negativity. If they are living in fear, if their lives are ruled by self-obsession, or if they cannot stop themselves from wanting more, it's clear that their success has not created true satisfaction and stability.

Understanding karma and cultivating virtue in order to bring about happiness is a very pragmatic approach. Karma itself is made from the mind. When we practice meditation, we stabilize the mind and try to reduce confusion. When the mind is agitated, it is more susceptible to self-absorption. But in meditating, we are not just learning to recognize major emotional upheavals; we are getting down to recognizing a very subtle level of fixation. We begin to see how when we regard ourselves as solid and permanent, we regard everything else as solid and permanent; that is what ignorance is. We begin to have glimpses of our primordial nature, which is open and free from duality—good and bad, virtue and nonvirtue.

With the right view, when negativity arises we can see it exactly for what it is, empty. My teachers used to ask me to try to find my emotions. Where is the anger? What color is it? What shape? When I practiced this contemplation, I discovered that I couldn't find my emotions, even though I could feel them. One would disappear, and another would arise. If we can truly see the nature of emotions as empty and not act on cravings, we can go beyond the obscuration of drip. That means not that we become robots but that we begin to see our mind and the world of appearances as vivid and fluid. Developing the view of basic goodness eventually has the power to free us from karma.

To affect the karma of our life at this very moment, we can choose to act with virtue. Knowing that the future depends on what we do right now, we can be discerning in our activity. As Padmasambhava once said, "My mind is vast like the sky, and my actions are subtle like sesame seeds." On the path of the tiger, our senses are open and we engage in life with appreciation and care about the decisions we make—not from fear of karma but out of respect for it. This view is the throne from which we begin to rule.

How can we liberate ourselves from karma? By ruling our mind. Whether in the privacy of our home or in public, we should feel good about why we are developing virtue. Treading the path of virtue is how we can finally take control of our life. However, first we have to understand that we are caught in karma's current. We've lost power over our mind. "Me" is blocking our view of basic goodness, and we keep acting from that ignorance. This is a result of previous confused action. We are currently creating negative karma, which adds to our confusion. That confusion will bear fruit in the future. Many elements of what might happen in the future are already in place, but with the tiger's mind, we can change the course of future karma. Discernment about what we are doing—payu—and knowledge about how things work—prajna—are vital, because tomorrow's chapter has not yet been written.

Whether a dandelion seed or a rock lands on our head, gravity neither laughs nor cries. In the same way, it doesn't matter to karma whether we're moving backward or forward. Whether we act virtuously or not, karma doesn't care. Knowing how karma works, we don't need to become more depressed or claustrophobic; nevertheless, we should realize that unless we rule our mind, there is no escape from confusion. When we wake up in the morning, we can ask ourselves, "Do I want to take control of my mind, or do I want to mindlessly create further scenarios that sow the seeds of fear?" If we infuse past karma with virtuous karma now, we can change the course of our life so that we're moving forward. By knowing how our mind works, we can gather virtue and use karma to create peace and happiness, which eventually lead to freedom. With appreciation, discernment, and exertion—the tools of the tiger—not only can we rule our life now but we can also rule our future.

6

The Utility of Regret

Regret shows us that we're not using the tiger in our life.

WHEN WE DON'T HAVE a clear strategy for living our life, making choices is bittersweet and stressful. We fear that if we miss an opportunity, later we'll have regret. This anxiety comes from experience. Sometimes we wake up in the middle of the night and talk to ourselves, so full of regret. If regret is very intense, we become angry. We're angry at ourselves for being stupid, for being a fool. Somebody took advantage of us. We thought we were getting a deal, so we bought a computer and then a better one came out. Why couldn't we have waited a few weeks?

Regret is a sign that we have acted without discernment. It causes mental hiccups that make us wince and cringe: "Why did I do that?" "I shouldn't have said that." "I shouldn't have bought that." "I should have turned off the television." "I shouldn't have eaten so much." "I should have stayed in school." "I should've said I loved you." "I should've said I'm sorry." A helpful antidote to discursive hiccups like these is appreciating how valuable our time is, and not wasting it on feeling regretful. We do not want to make regret a theme of our life.

I have been with many people as they neared death. This is always a powerful time. Their words may reflect confusion, fear, anger, denial, or acceptance. One of the most powerful statements someone in this state can make is that he or she has no regrets. By contrast, we can feel the worst kind of regret at the end of our life. It's a haunting and frightening space, knowing that we had 365 days in every single year to change our attitude. We realize we have had thousands upon thousands of days on which we missed our opportunity to live life with discernment and appreciation.

My predecessor Mipham the Great was one of the most revered lamas in Tibet. He wrote thirty-two seminal works that changed how Buddhism was taught and practiced there. His writings now bring joy to people everywhere, inspiring them to find true meaning in their lives by helping others. He spent much of his life in meditation retreats, and he remains famous for writing on a broad spectrum of topics, from metaphysics to tantra. He was a true Renaissance man—he even drew pictures describing how to make airplanes and cars. He wrote major medical and astrology texts, and he also wrote extensively on Gesar of Ling, the legendary Tibetan king. Mipham was the teacher of kings, princes, and all the high lamas of his time. When he was dying, he said that, now that his work was done, he was going to go to Shambhala, where he would manifest as a compassionate ruler to help overcome the dark age of the setting sun. Because he had led a life dedicated to others, he was free from regret.

It is said that if our intention is to help others—even if we are unable to follow it through—we will never have any regret. Regret is a result of trying to make "me" happy. It shows us that we're not using the tiger in our life. Payu went on holiday. Discernment took a break. Our mind checked out. Bewilderment came back onstage. We didn't pay attention to what the world was telling us. We made a faulty decision based on anger, jealousy, desire, or pride—signs that we are looking out for "me." If anger is the cause and we want happiness as the result, it's not going to work, because every result has to have a relationship to the cause.

By contemplating the preciousness of human life, the law of karma, the suffering of samsara, the truth of impermanence, and the compassion and wisdom that are true freedom, we learn to think accurately. We usually don't pay attention to these truths until our expectations about life are interrupted by aches in our body or lines on our face, an accident, or the illness or death of somebody close to us. Then we experience a moment of panic that temporarily cuts through drip, our web of habitual assumptions. We don't want to dwell in that open space, so our next move is usually to find a way back to the false security of "me." We don't think, "Life is precious. I'd better start helping others." We just go back to pursuing pleasure or not rocking the boat. Thinking we have all the time in the world, we waste it. Our decisions are based on inaccurate information rooted in hope. We are lazy and unfocused, which corrupts our behavior and eventually leads to regret.

It's never too late to change our mind, but when we find ourselves on our deathbed, it's too late to change our life. Reflecting back, we wish we had taken notice and done something more meaningful. When I meet with people who are dying, this is the overriding message I hear. Some are afraid of dying and others are not, but most people wish they had noticed earlier how precious life was; most people wish they had used it better. Most people wish they had been kinder to others, loved others more. Nobody says, "If only I had been jealous and angry more often."

Contemplation is the most powerful tool we have for changing our behavior. By choosing to direct our thoughts toward seeing clearly how things really are, we convince ourselves to try another way of living. Contemplating the truth is a practice of imagining we are lying on our deathbed every morning and thinking earnestly about how we can live our life in sync with reality.

At the end of every day, we can again imagine that we are that dying person. Can we look back on only one day and say that we have no regrets? We can just think about what we did that day, and what's occurring in our life. Then we can watch little thoughts of regret float to the top of our mind like flotsam from a sunken ship: "I wish I had—or had not—done such-and-such." Regret is retroactive attachment. It's thinking that something or someone else was more worthy of doing or wanting. Regretting our relationship with someone implies a lack of love and appreciation.

Often when we have regret, it is difficult to reflect on what led to it, because it's too painful. We barge ahead, and a few weeks later we find ourselves feeling regretful about the same thing. Nothing has changed. If we are to change our behavior and move our life forward, we need to take heed of regret. We need to acknowledge it and articulate our intention to do better. Contemplating regret doesn't require being moralistic or getting into heavy penance. Without chastising ourselves, we just look at regret as clearly as we can. We use the intelligence of regret as a barometer that shows us how we're leading our life.

When something doesn't feel right, we can contemplate it. What was our attitude when it happened? That attitude is now causing us pain in the form of regret, and it might have hurt another person, too. Would it help to clarify, to apologize? How would we like to do things differently? The point is to learn as much as possible from the feeling of regret.

In this spirit, we make a conscious decision to come back to the path of the tiger and lead our life with appreciation and discernment. We are making a promise to ourselves. In Tibet, people seal this aspiration with a physical act. They make a lamp from butter and place it on a shrine before an image of the Buddha or the picture of another teacher. They might offer some incense. In Tibet, butter and incense are valuable commodities. People don't waste them. Making such offerings demonstrates a serious intent to change direction. The lamp signifies coming out of the darkness of the "me" plan. Its light represents an aspiration to exit the tunnel of self-preservation and illuminate our life with wisdom. The incense symbolizes the sweet smell of a life lived for the benefit of others.

We too should stop, acknowledge our regret, and take the next step toward ruling our world. We could mark the moment with a ritual as simple or as involved as we wish, resolving to improve our conduct and become more mature. Then we can rise in the morning intending to make it a regret-free day by exerting ourselves in discernment and putting others first.

People say, "I want to help others, but I have to get my life together first." I'm saying that you need to eat well, sleep well, and have a roof over your head, but don't go much further than that before extending yourself to others. It doesn't work. If we want any level of happiness, we must put others' concerns before ourselves. We may think it's a choice, but in reality, it's choiceless. Decision by decision, putting others first is how we begin to conquer agitation and raise windhorse, the ability to bring about success and happiness. Otherwise, throughout our day we are planting seeds of regret that will blossom in pain, discomfort, and anxiety.

When we are certain that the way to accomplish our own

wishes is to help others, we have no regrets. We are not looking at our possessions regretting that we bought them. We are not looking at our partner regretting that we married her. We are not looking at our job regretting that we started it. What is life free from regret? It is the confidence of the tiger—contentment. It comes from leading our life with appreciation of our good fortune, and extending that sense of peace and well-being to others.

7

The Virtue of Exertion

*Exerting ourselves toward virtue creates stability
in our lives—happiness that we can depend on.*

P EOPLE OFTEN ASK ME why I seem so happy. They
think that I must have some kind of secret. I do—exertion. Not that I'm a perfect example of this virtue, but it's
easy for me to see that the joy I feel doesn't come from lying
around doing nothing, or having no responsibilities. It has to
do with deciding what I want to do and engaging in it wholeheartedly.

When I began running, my students often assumed I had
a yogic secret that I apply to my training. In fact, I am simply
using the same principles in my running that I apply in meditation. Even though running is a physical activity, it mostly
has to do with exerting the mind. One of my main strategies
is to engage my mind completely. I want to run, so I get up

early in the day to do it, before beginning my schedule. It isn't that difficult, because I have decided to exert myself. When I'm running, I practice placing my mind on my stride, my posture, or my breath, acknowledging thoughts as they arise and bringing my mind back to what I'm doing.

Exertion is necessary to accomplish anything—spiritual or worldly. When people visit me at Namdroling monastery in India, they come expecting some kind of utopia where everybody meditates all the time. They are always surprised to see how busy the monastery is. From very early in the morning until late at night, the monks are chanting, meditating, studying, cooking food, and washing dishes.

Often people in the monastic college debate the merits of prajna—best knowledge—versus exertion. Although it is best to have both, everybody always decides that exertion is more important, because with exertion, we can do anything. Nothing is out of reach. Without exertion, having payu—discernment—and prajna is like having a boat with no paddles. Knowing what to do is not enough; we have to do it. In Tibet we say, "The peak of a mountain is not too high and the bottom of the ocean is not too deep as long as you have exertion." Without discernment, however, we can waste our time endlessly and make things even worse by exerting ourselves in the wrong direction. After all, we could be quite engaged in exerting ourselves in negativity. We could be exerting ourselves full speed ahead in making a weapon to hurt someone. We could be exerting ourselves in contemplating how to get revenge. The exertion of the king and queen is thoroughly engaged in moving forward on the path of virtue, which leads to joy.

Exerting ourselves toward virtue means exerting ourselves toward getting off the "me" plan and getting into thinking of the welfare of others. We start by exerting ourselves toward finding peace in our own mind. This begins to happen in breathing meditation. In contemplation, we cultivate awareness that allows us to see clearly how things are in a relative way. We begin to see our actions and the results of our actions. We see clearly what our negative karmic actions can produce. We decide not to clean the floor, and somebody trips and falls. We forget to bring the patio cushions inside, and they get wet in the rain.

We can then exert ourselves in extending peace and insight into our daily life—not always wanting more than we have, not being seduced by anger and pride, taking a vacation from our speed, and making room for others. That means exerting ourselves in patience when we feel angry, and in generosity when we're feeling attached. This can be as simple as watching angry thoughts arise and fall without giving voice to them. We can let our grudge wear itself out rather than perpetuate the negativity by acting on it.

Most of us are not interested in exerting ourselves toward virtue, because we are still not inspired by it. Inspiration may not come in one fell swoop. It helps to look for examples. Our friend the single mother, who is patient with her children even after a long day's work, can be an inspiration. Our grandfather, who adapts to changing circumstances with relentless cheerfulness, might be a good example. The former CEO who makes headlines by simplifying his life and devoting himself to teaching underprivileged children can inspire us. I do not know of a single teacher of high wisdom and compassion who does not exude exertion. They have overcome self-centeredness, rendering it rubble with exertion.

On the path of the tiger, exertion is the moment that follows payu—discernment. Having decided to take the direction of virtue, we move forward with joy. This joy comes from the contentment of knowing what we are exerting ourselves for. Anything is difficult when we're not sure we want to be doing it. Having made a decision, we follow it with one-pointed attention. Paradoxically, this may mean slowing down to engage fully in our activity. With the stealth of the tiger, we give ourselves time to focus and allow our senses to absorb what we are doing. This moment makes the difference between just seeing a flower and appreciating it.

We can make almost any hill flat with exertion, because we're excited to run up it. By contrast, without exertion, even walking down a flat road is difficult. There are differences in elevation, of course, but the real difference lies not in the road but in our mind. Subconsciously we know that we're on the wrong path. Lack of exertion—and lack of joy—is laziness. Laziness reduces the possibility of bringing about happiness. Exertion liberates us from laziness, and takes us toward joy.

We all want joy in our lives, but we often go about seeking it in a backward way. We fool ourselves into thinking that pleasure lies in not applying ourselves. Even though we cannot really take a break from life, we keep trying. We're finally on our dream vacation, and we just want to flop. Without structure and plans, however, we never really enjoy ourselves. When we don't make the effort to reserve seats at a restaurant or to learn how to scuba dive, there is that much less joy. We need to rest at times, of course, but exertion is natural. The mind needs to engage. We naturally want meaning in our life.

In contemplating exertion, we may draw the conclusion that we don't have much of it. But if we look at the landscape of our lives with the eyes of the tiger and ask, "What am I exerting myself toward?" we'll see that, in fact, we are practicing exertion all the time—often in the wrong direction. We exert ourselves toward scheming how we're going to make things work out for "me." We exert ourselves in venting our anger. We exert ourselves toward finding a little pleasure to temporarily ease our pain. We use it to try to have fun. Ironically, with exertion, we don't need to go out to have fun. We can have fun inside.

Sometimes in India, we would ask the old masters if we could leave the monastery to have a few hours off. Our teachers would smile and agree to our request, but in such a way that we would wonder what they meant. We thought that maybe they were old and had forgotten how to have a good time. Then we would go out and try to have fun, always with mixed results.

After years of practice and study, I've begun to understand why those realized teachers don't need to go out to have fun. It's not that they are antisocial or afraid of the world. They already have what everybody else wants and is looking for—contentment and joy. However, theirs are of a more permanent variety. They may not have seen the latest movie or eaten at the trendy new place, but they know that movies and restaurants come and go. They know that ultimately it is not food that brings about the relaxation from which satisfaction and joy arise. It is exerting ourselves toward a meaningful life, developing confidence in basic goodness, and expressing it with wisdom and compassion.

When we hear about our potential for ruling our world, the number one factor that makes it seem impossible is lack of exertion. When people ask me how they could hold the view of basic goodness, be compassionate, and manifest wisdom, what is written across their faces is doubt. Exertion would render that doubt powerless. When exertion arises, doubt—which manifests as drip—disappears.

What are the mountains in our lives that exertion can climb? The steepest hill is no higher than one step. As I've learned in running, having exertion for that one step can make any mountain flat. With exertion, we can conquer aggression. How many times do we really apply ourselves toward overcoming anger? Meditating helps us clear the space in our mind to see it, which is a step in the right direction. Contemplating karma inspires us to work with it. The process of overcoming it is exertion. As rulers, we know that our greatest treasure is our ability to exert ourselves toward virtue. Exerting ourselves toward virtue creates stability in our lives—happiness that we can depend on.

8

Hanging Out
with the Right Crowd

The tiger knows that life is precious. Whom are we going to spend it with?

W E MAY WAKE UP with confidence in basic goodness, but unless we are the Buddha, our view is going to change throughout the day. Unless our friends Fred and Mary Jane are the Buddha, their view is always going to be changing, too. Who are we going to listen to, Fred and Mary Jane, or the Buddha? The Buddha wakes up and goes to bed every day with the same view. Even if we woke him up in the middle of the night, his view would still be the same. This isn't because he's stubborn or opinionated; it's because his view is based on certainty in the reality of basic goodness, rather than on certainty in the concept of "me."

In making friends, we are cultivating the influence of each other's view. If we want to rule our world, we need to be mindful about who we're hanging out with and aware of their influence. Fred and Mary Jane are sitting on the couch eating potato chips and clicking the remote control, and we think, "Oh, that looks like fun, let's try it." At work, our friend uses lunch as an occasion to gossip about other people on the staff, and after a while, we begin to take pleasure in that. Our best friend yells at his children, and we start to do it, too.

At this early stage of training, even though we aspire to use discernment in our conduct, we're sometimes not able to hold the view of the tiger when we're with others. We forget about karma. Our mind dribbles. Our windhorse weakens. Our discernment slowly wanes, and we fail to exert ourselves. Drip thickens our view, and we forget the meaning of our life. Our compassion diminishes. If we're always hanging our with the wrong crowd, after a while we don't think twice about following the example of our friends—even stealing or hurting our family—and our noble qualities are totally eclipsed. It is difficult to connect with windhorse in an environment that encourages nonvirtue.

However, if our friends conduct themselves in a positive way, they have a positive influence. We think, "Wow. Fred was really angry, but he let it go. Maybe I could let go, too." Or "Mary Jane doesn't seem to speed around as much since she started meditating. Maybe I should try it." The teachings tell us that it's better to have one virtuous friend than a thousand bad ones.

The king and queen regard everyone as a friend, because their confidence in basic goodness is indestructible. Their intention is always to generate compassion. They can extend the wish-fulfilling jewel of wisdom and compassion even toward a pigeon that has just left droppings on the windshield of their car. The rest of us, however, are still caught in the unstable mind of "me." Even though we may be getting glimpses of peace and stability in our daily practice, our budding windhorse is like a child taking its first steps.

To help it thrive, we must be discerning about our mental and physical environment. The Shambhala teachings instruct us to put ourselves in the "cradle of loving-kindness." On the path of the tiger, we begin with kindness toward ourselves, which means cultivating thoughts and friends that strengthen windhorse. Appreciating our life and the influence of others, we look at our relationships with the eyes of the tiger. Hanging out with the wrong crowd, be it the crowd of thoughts in our head or the people we call friends, only reinforces discursiveness and negativity. Nonvirtuous companions are like termites that eat away our noble qualities. The tiger knows that life is precious. Who are we going to spend it with?

If we're led around by negative emotions, we're likely to choose friends with whom we can get cozy in a small world of shared complaints, shared dislikes, shared desires. In choosing who we hang out with, what is our attitude? Are we shoring up the citadel of "me"? Or do we look for a deeper basis of friendship?

In sitting practice, we're using the mind's natural clarity to start our day with the right friend. We're creating a less hassled atmosphere, an environment that is free from distracting marauders that provoke knee-jerk reactions like jealousy and competition. We're hanging out with the Buddha, which is like listening to a good friend who is telling us the truth. Even though we sometimes squirm and want to walk away, we decide to stick around, because we recognize that, no matter how uncomfortable we may feel, our friend has our best interests at heart. We can use that natural strength to remind us every day of who we are—goodness.

There is a blue buddha known as Samantabhadra, the all-good. Blue represents the basic nature of all beings, like a cloudless sky. That blue we see when we look high up—that's who we are. When we rest in the natural energy of our mind, doubt and hesitation evaporate, and we can experience that goodness. Like the sky, it's empty; therefore it can accommodate everything. Hesitating about who we really are or hanging out with the wrong friends—whether they are people or the negativity in our mind—is like the clouds. We see clouds and take them to be real, but behind the clouds the sun is shining, illuminating the world. The Great Eastern Sun is our own wisdom. The more we choose to trust and nourish it, the less influenced we are by the clouds.

As we stabilize our certainty in basic goodness, we are able to extend ourselves to others with genuine purpose. One of the Tibetan words for friend means "helper." In Tibet, the first thing we do upon meeting someone is to offer this intention in the form of a white scarf that symbolizes friendship. We greet everyone with the hope and wish of helping them first. The thought of helping others is compassion, knowing how we can do it is wisdom, and doing something about it is courage. The wish-fulfilling jewel of wisdom and compassion is the basis of true friendship.

Sometimes we are like children sitting on the playground wishing we had more friends. But if we dwell in this immature state—wanting to get, unwilling to give—having friends becomes difficult. We lack the basic currency of friendship. Trying to rule our world through selfishness doesn't work, because we are taking, not giving. Once we take, others take from us. Under such conditions, none of us is able to gather virtue. In helping our friends, we accomplish their wishes as well as our own. Helping our friends increases their ability and willingness to help us.

Friendship is derailed when we stop helping our helper, because we're treating it as a one-way street headed toward "me." When people ask me about their personal relationships, I can read the future simply by the attitude of the question. If they talk about what the other person is not doing for them, I know the relationship is probably doomed. If I hear, "I need more support, I need more love, I need more attention. My concerns have to be understood," I take it as a sign that the friendship has collapsed. These are symptoms of desperation. Although it may all be true, they have forgotten that friendship takes two. They are unable to accommodate the ups and downs of relationship. Friendship is based upon karma. If you help the other person, your friendship develops. If you are totally self-absorbed, your marriage is not going to last.

To create a lasting relationship requires continual discernment and exertion. It means thinking about what we are willing to give before looking at how much we are going to get. As difficult and unjust as it may sometimes seem, if we are to be a true friend, we should always be thinking, "What can I do for my friend?" "How can I support her?" "How can I care for him more?" For this reason, before we engage in a friendship, we should reflect on what it will ask of us and make sure we can follow through on that commitment.

With this attitude, friendship becomes a spiritual practice, one which teaches us that we can be strong, accommodating, and generous. Our kindness creates a field of power—*wangthang*—a quality of genuine presence that grows from our intimacy with virtue. The more peaceful, cheerful, and generous we are, the more successful we are in attracting friends, as well as everything else we need.

The enlightened king and queen are friends to everyone, because they have a fierce commitment to their welfare. Spiritual friends like this are selfless, infused with compassion. They help others help themselves. Not only do they lead people in the right direction, but they always have others' best interests in mind. They see even an enemy as a future friend. When we live in a meaningful way and inspire others in the same direction, we too can be spiritual friends. Being this kind of friend requires the humility of the tiger: we know that in working with others, we are working with ourselves.

How do we rule the world? By making friends with it. Thus, a useful contemplation on the path of the tiger is, How can I be a true friend to myself and others? What should I cultivate and what should I discard? In contemplating questions like these, we are inviting our heart to open. This is how to be a friend as soon as we arise.

9

The Confidence of Contentment

Moving through our life with the steady vigilance of a tiger, we no longer feel the need to prove ourselves, because we know the truth of our own peace.

THE BUDDHA TAUGHT that suffering is a result of roaming, the urge to keep looking for an external source of happiness. In Tibetan, a word for human beings is *drowa*—"movers." We wander not out of delight but out of discontent. The place that we're looking for, where happiness lies, is contentment. In a restaurant, we might look over and see somebody eating a delicious-looking salad, a nice juicy steak, a piece of pizza dripping with cheese, or some double chocolate cake with whipped cream and berries. We turn to the waiter and say, "I want that." When it arrives, it somehow doesn't taste as good as we'd imagined. It wasn't the food we wanted—it was the contentment we saw in that other person.

Much of our stress these days is caused by a simple lack of

contentment. In my constant travels, from the highland meadows of Tibet to the tropical rain forest of Brazil to the busy streets of Hong Kong, I've learned that you have to be content wherever you are. Otherwise, traveling is exhausting, because you're always thinking that the next place will be better. Sometimes the people who travel with me—although they are young and energetic—burn out, because they are not content. They spend their energy hoping that the bed or the meal will improve somewhere down the road.

Even if we don't travel from country to country, our mind is always moving. We think that contentment is going to be found in one more bite of food, one more word, one more round of golf, one more glass of wine, one more item of clothing, one more kiss. How much of the day do we spend in this ordinary pursuit? We have a meeting with desire at six in the morning, and again at ten, and a lunch date with desire, and definitely drinks, then dinnertime with dessert—the biggest desire—and even a midnight snack. Somehow in the midst of all this, we have to relax, stop grazing, and be content. Otherwise, we exhaust ourselves with the ambition of always moving on to the next desire.

If we don't know how to be content in our mind, we can't even be content with our food. Eating at the best restaurant in the world won't make any difference. There is someone in a village in India eating curry out of a clay bowl, more content than we are. When we find the pair of shoes we want, for a brief moment we feel content. But when that moment passes, we're on the move again: food doesn't taste good, clothes don't fit, the sheets are too rough, the bath's not hot enough. We need better movies, more exciting books, a new relationship. We need to live on a different planet.

Desire is a creature with an endless appetite. Like a spark put to dry grass, it just consumes. By its very nature, it can never be satisfied, because it is rooted in the aggression of looking outside ourselves for relief. That expectation always results in disappointment, self-generated pain. It's the mind giving itself a hard time. Seeing how we give ourselves a hard time is intelligence. The result of payu—knowing when to stop—is contentment. This kind of contentment gives us dignity. Walking mindfully with discernment, possessing tremendous exertion, we are meek and gentle, because we know we already have everything we need. We have discovered our mind's peace, and we have a plan for living our life. This contentment is the confidence of the tiger. It is called "confidence" because it stabilizes the mind and quells the aggression of wanting things to be anything but what they are.

The Shambhala teachings say that the confidence of contentment arises from being friendly to ourselves and merciful to others. Friendliness to ourselves is a result of meditation. When we have learned to practice meditation properly, we are no longer struggling with our mind. Our mind is content because it is no longer stolen by ordinary activity—the meaningless fantasy of "What about me?" Self-reflection and payu have given us some distance from our projections. No longer are we paupers looking for the next crumb of confirmation, because we have discovered the peace that lies beneath that agitation. We are not rehashing what happened in the past; we are not thinking about what we could do in the future; we are acting now.

If we are able to see what to cultivate and what to discard—even as we work with our own thought patterns—then we are inviting the drala of contentment. We are practicing the basis of an enlightened world: the ability to see our aggression, to discern what the result of that agitation could be, and to make another choice. We think twice before acting with irritation or ambition. That might mean taking a deep breath, not honking the car horn, counting to ten before speaking, or saving the draft of an angry e-mail instead of pressing Send. At that moment, instead of creating the kingdom of fear, the kingdom of arrogance, or the kingdom of animosity, we are deciding to radiate another kind of energy. Because we have confidence in our own peace, we can dwell in the kingdom of contentment. The more we trust our peace, the more we see that it is very potent. With that sense of contentment, negativity is easier to disperse. It has the power to take us beyond fear. The result is complete friendliness—harmony and lack of agitation. We are no longer creating tension.

Mercy is having enough friendliness with our own mind to see someone else's predicament. At this point, being merciful to others is very much a conscious decision. It comes from knowing what happens if we do not have mercy: we act with aggression. We use spiteful words, or knowingly engage in behavior that denigrates someone else. Now we see clearly that if we lie, lash out, or react with jealousy, we feel contaminated, heavy, and defensive, as if we are trying to validate ourselves. When we do this, we can feel our windhorse weaken. This tells us that our mind has slipped into ordinary activity, a symptom that we are no longer content.

Payu reminds us that we do not have to be fooled by our

own projections. We can choose to act with care. When we make a decision according to the law of karma, we are synchronized with the ways of the world. We are modest and therefore without pride. We do not pounce out of reactivity. We are not on the prowl for attention or entertainment. We know that fixation leads to suffering. We know that having more doesn't necessarily bring pleasure. That is how we release ourselves from the fetters of aggression.

Every time we step beyond aggression, we gain *ziji*—inner confidence—an understanding that is beyond emotional intelligence. Moving through our life with the steady vigilance of a tiger, we no longer feel the need to prove ourselves, because we are anchored in the truth of our own peace. Beautiful new clothes, a promotion at work, or climbing Mount Everest might bring pleasure, but they are not going to make that peace any bigger.

The contentment that payu brings is like being lost and then finally knowing how to get out of the woods. No longer do we use deception as a tool, because we're not engaged in an ongoing battle of self-preservation. We are not leading our life trying to bolster ourselves up with pleasure or hide from our own pain. For example, we often talk ourselves into thinking we are having a good time on the "me" plan. The notion of overcoming deception is to be totally honest about that. It is not necessary to wake up on our deathbed with the realization that we were not having a good time and that we were afraid to do something different.

With the contentment of the tiger, we have not given up on life—far from it. Meditation reveals the pattern of short-term gain and loss, and payu points us toward longer-term rewards. This doesn't mean that we don't enjoy a game of football or try to do our best at whatever we undertake. We take it all in stride. On the path of rulership, we are engaging in our worldly life in an unconventional way. We are not looking for rewards such as gain; we are not looking for high-maintenance victory. We know that all gain turns to loss; all pleasure turns to pain. By expanding our confidence in basic goodness, we learn to trust ourselves, and we give up trying to succeed with ambition or aggression. Eventually, we even give up attachment to pain and pleasure, hope and fear.

The self-assured strength that grows from knowing that we already have what we need makes us gentle. We are gentle because we are no longer desperate. We might associate gentleness with being demure or afraid. On the contrary, lack of aggression is the fruition of the tiger's path. It comes from the insight that being pushy makes things harder. Studying in Nepal with Tulku Ugyen, one of the great old teachers from Tibet, I was tremendously affected by something he told me: "Being aggressive, you can accomplish some things, but with gentleness, you can accomplish all things."

When we approach a situation in a meek and humble way, the blessing energy of drala is there to help. Sacredness begins to shine through the world as the richness of the Rigden— our own awareness. Our senses—taste, touch, sight, smell, sound—take on a higher quality. There is a strong sense of appreciation. That sense of appreciation is coming from a mind that is much more able to appreciate, because it is content.

III

THE PATH
OF THE LION

10

The Virtue of Discipline

> The discipline of the lion allows windhorse to
> arise, which brings energy and delight.

WHEN I'M ON RETREAT in India, I keep a very disciplined schedule. The early morning gong goes off around four, and I can hear the drums beginning for the morning liturgy. Young monks are chanting, and in other parts of the monastery, people are doing their early morning meditations. There's an atmosphere of discipline and energy. When I'm back in the West, people ask me if being in India at the monastery is difficult. It's true that we go for periods without electricity or water, that sometimes it's very hot, that there are many strange insects, and that the food is simple. But because I'm engaged in something that I want to do and enjoy doing, I'm always happy to be there.

The path of the tiger has shown us that discernment and

exertion bring peace. Not only that, but it is satisfying to have a plan for our life. On the path of the lion, we use the precision of discipline to increase our joy. Without discipline, the small mind of "me" takes over, because that's our long-established habit. Our mind begins to drift. When we have no direction, it's hard to be content. We become edgy, anxious, or depressed. We become sloppy, which affects our mental alertness. We become dull and unexpressive in our communication and less productive in our work. We study, yet we don't learn. Our colleagues feel as if we are dragging them down. With discipline, we are making a container in which we can continue to grow. Only through discipline can we truly experience our vast mind, the outer limits of our possibilities.

Tibetan *tulkus*—incarnate lamas who choose to be reborn in order to help others—were held in the highest esteem, but they were brought up under the strictest of conditions. In Tibet, there's a saying, "Gold and tulkus must be beaten." Unless gold is pounded out, its purity is simply raw potential, never fully utilized. Great teachers like my father and others of the older generation have been very matter-of-fact about how strictly they were disciplined in their upbringing. If their tutors hadn't been strict, these teachers wouldn't have had such deep development and understanding. At the same time, without exception they are delightful people.

This strictness carried into my own training as a sakyong. Once my father instructed me to do a series of meditations that would require one long year of practice. A year later, I enthusiastically told him that I had completed the practice. When he heard this, he told me to go do it again. He said, "You will always have to do twice as much as everybody else, because in the future you will have to lead people. Therefore you need to be worthy." At the time, it was hard to accept his response. However, I found that practicing this way made me feel confident, as though I could accomplish anything. The discipline of the practice helped me tame my mind. My mind had made a leap. I had more perspective on what I was doing and why.

Connecting to a larger view, we begin to conquer small-mindedness. No longer is our mind so cluttered by negativity, thick with drip. We keep meditating, contemplating, and trying to apply virtue in our daily life because doing so seems to make a difference. Our life is making more sense. At first perhaps it felt like drudgery to stick with our training, but now we do it because we enjoy it. The discipline of the lion allows windhorse to arise, which brings energy and delight.

With the discipline to engage in virtue and to stay with it, enjoyment comes naturally. In traffic, we notice that slowing down to give the parking spot to someone else feels less stressful than stepping on the gas to get there first. At work, we see that being patient instead of angry when a project takes longer than scheduled actually gives us more energy to complete it. Before, virtue was a theory, a place that we had heard about. Now we have experienced it firsthand. Abiding by the laws of karma has brought us the confidence of contentment. We know that virtue is the way to go. We see how not harming ourselves and others frees us from confusion. We feel lighter, as if our internal brilliance is buoying us up.

This levity is *nyingje*—compassion, "noble heart." When our nobility is liberated, compassion and love flow freely. There's an uplifted quality to our being, because we have risen above aggression. We are no longer caught in the trap of doubt. Doubt is that part of the mind that is obscuring our wisdom. Its expressions—anxiety, jealousy, ambition, aggression, forgetfulness, and pride—hide our basic goodness and make the mind less flexible. When we are liberated from the trap of doubt, our mind is bigger and compassion flows naturally. We can incorporate any situation without a struggle.

I have seen this open-hearted quality in the great teachers that I have studied with, including my father. People often remember him for his crazy-wisdom energy, but having been with him day in and day out, I remember someone who was very gentle, loving, and kind. I have had the same experience with my teachers Khyentse Rinpoche and Penor Rinpoche; they exude gentleness and joy because they do not struggle with reality. This is a result of their discipline. Having completely conquered their own aggression, they devote their lives to awakening others to the truth of basic goodness. Proclaiming this truth is known as the "lion's roar."

By far the best way to conquer aggression is to think of others. At tax time, for example, if we remember that others are suffering the same panic, worry, or irritation, it softens our agitation. When we're ill, thinking of others who are also sick dissolves our claustrophobia and fear. Thinking of others connects us with our noble heart. When we maintain this connection, we are patient with our own suffering. We're not derailed by negativity, because compassion has expanded our mind, and "me" looks smaller. We're no longer eyeing the world jealously with the view that we're the only ones who suffer. We know that everybody suffers.

Thinking of others is the lion's discipline. We are delighted to help others, because when we do, we can feel our heart rising above self-absorption. With that kind of delight, we are no longer lowly beings, caught in the valley bottom—hesitant, doubtful, not understanding the purpose of life. We are high on the mountain, knowing why we're here and which direction we want to go. In the flag of Tibet, the snow lion is holding up the sun, which represents having confidence in our own nobility. Our hearts are cheerful, because we appreciate our own wisdom. Because we do not confuse what we should accept with what we should reject, our body and mind are healthy and youthful. With this kind of confidence, we are frolicking in the highlands, where the air is clean and the water is pure, leaping from mountain to mountain through the clouds. It is said that the snow lion lives in meadows that are teeming with wildflowers and fragrant air. This means that when we practice virtue, we ourselves smell sweet, for virtue is the strongest of perfumes. Like snow lions, we revel in this high-mindedness. We're not high because of arrogance—we are high because we know why we are using virtue in our life, and where it is taking us. Bringing purpose to our life is taking us above the pauper's jealousy. This discipline brings delight.

Because of our discipline, we no longer enter the lower realms of negativity. We are uplifted and joyful in whatever we do, and our actions are graceful and splendidly accomplished. Having dared to make this crucial leap, we can enjoy the fruits of the higher realms—long life, good health, a good body, good luck, good family, wealth, and prajna—that continue to liberate our noble heart. When our compassion is unfettered, we can act on it, extending joy to all.

11

No Blame

There is always something to complain about; blaming others is not going to bring about peace or happiness.

RECENTLY I WAS STUCK in the security lineup at an airport. Everybody was upset because our luggage was being X-rayed so slowly. People were putting themselves into an increasingly agitated state, blaming the security personnel for making us late. Obviously, the staff were just trying to do their jobs, and ultimately, we didn't solve any problems by blaming them for the hassles of travel these days. I realized that we could just as easily be blaming people who want to blow up airplanes, who are themselves blaming someone else—and the wheel rolls on. It seems like the world is becoming too small a place for everyone to be wielding blame. Where can it all go?

When we're disappointed or frustrated, when we're in pain, or when our day's not going well—these are times when we're likely to forget about the lion's discipline and delight, and search for an object of blame. Our backbone softens, and our heart hardens. Our mantra becomes "If it weren't for you, I wouldn't be having this problem." The ruler knows that blame is tricky. We believe someone stole our joy, and that becomes our view. When we blame, we are failing to deal with our own mind. We're hardening our frustration and jealousy into a little ball and throwing it at somebody else. The minute we say, "It's your fault!" we are abdicating the throne of our mind.

That moment shows that our discernment, exertion, contentment, and discipline are still conditioned by having things go our way. We can't hold the royal view of certainty in basic goodness, so we abandon it. Having walked away from our stability and strength, we become paupers, jealous that someone or something has stolen our peace, and projecting our helplessness outward: "If only the driver in front of me had been going faster, I wouldn't be late for work." "If only someone else had cleaned the kitchen, I would be watching my favorite TV show instead of doing these dishes." Even if we find someone we can logically blame for our pain, conducting our life with complaint does not provide genuine relief. Blaming and complaining just lay the ground for further discontent. Looking for an object to which we can attach our negativity and irritation destroys our discipline. We forget all about the highland meadows of the lion and sink into the swamp of "me."

By blaming others when the world does not move the way we want, we are creating narrow parameters into which everything must fit. We become dead set on what we think will solve our problem; nothing else will do. Blame ties us to the past and makes our mind smaller. It dampens our delight and limits our possibilities. What is blame going to accomplish? In this dark age, when it's so easy to blame other countries, other cultures, other ways of thinking, blame will only exasperate any situation. Even when we experience an acutely painful event and feel completely justified in pointing the finger of blame, we are choosing to make ourselves smaller. We are ingraining our meditation on "What about me?"

As long as we're looking for someone to blame, we are unable to stay on the path of the lion, because our mind is unable to settle. Through meditation, we acknowledge the activity of our mind in a very pragmatic way. This is an opportunity to observe the activity of blame. Rather than radiate negativity, we can see that the real source of our discontent is our unwillingness to work with our mind. As long as we are looking for a place to attach blame and complaint, we are ignoring the possibility of using discipline to see confusion for what it is.

Instead of looking for a place to attach our blame, we could be using our mind to understand that aggression itself is an expression of suffering. If we develop the self-awareness to realize this, we will no longer be hooked into the habit of blame. We don't need to become masochistic and blame ourselves; we need to realize that pain and suffering—no matter what kind of day we are having—are a very basic reality. We can acknowledge that we are having a difficult time; we are in pain. That acknowledgment opens our heart and mind to the reality of compassion. No matter who we find to blame, that individual also is in pain.

The Buddha outlined four basic truths. *Truth* means relevant for everyone—not true for some and not for others, or true on some days and not the rest. The first truth is the truth of suffering. He said, "Everyone is suffering because they are clinging to this idea called 'me.' When things are taken away, we get angry. When things are given, we become attached. We are jealous when others have more than we do. This clinging makes karma, which keeps us in an endless cycle of dissatisfaction." We think about that, and we draw the conclusion that negative emotions keep us in a cycle of suffering. Drawing this conclusion inspires us to remember the discipline of the lion, which comes from having a sense of purpose.

We live in a world where suffering is the constant. If we find pain in our life, we shouldn't be shocked, or take it as a personal insult. We haven't failed as human beings if we suffer. In fact, suffering lays the ground for compassion—consideration for others and ourselves. Everybody has bad days, everybody has difficulties, and blaming somebody else is not going to change that truth. Blaming is a way of running from that truth. When we take the path of blame, each complaint lays the ground for the next, and nothing gets any better. Thus the cycle continues. That is the meaning of the word *samsara*—circular, always feeling the rub of suffering and then looking for a way to make it go away.

The remedy for samsara is a reality check. There is always something to complain about; blaming others for that is not going to bring peace or happiness. If we can relax our mind instead of blaming, we might see the humor in how the world works. We will remember that underneath it all, we are already happy. Recognizing, acknowledging, and releasing thoughts by bringing our mind back to the object of meditation helps remind us that the frantic agitation of blame is unnatural and temporary. The wisdom and love beneath the clutter of negativity are natural and permanent.

In discovering this space, we are spawning a new relationship to our life. We are switching tracks. The maturity we develop by following the path of virtue gives us the base by which we can feel compassion for others instead of blaming them. Instead of obsessing on our own satisfaction, we begin to see what is going on with others. We can see that the person we are blaming needs help, and so we help him. Helping him reduces our desire to blame, and increases our desire to be of benefit.

This is how life becomes joyful. We are relieving our mind of the burden of blame, no longer draining our life-force energy in a fight with the environment. We are coming out of our shell of self-obsession, breaking free from our preconception of how things ought to be. Not blaming doesn't make us docile, just accepting whatever comes along. It allows us to open our heart to suffering instead of closing it with blame.

I have heard my father and others of the older generation of Tibetan lamas saying that they did not blame the Communist Chinese for the destruction of Tibet. They felt that blaming the Chinese would not solve anything. It would only trap Tibetans in the past. As the Dalai Lama has said, the Chinese invasion became a teacher, a powerful challenge for increasing compassion, an opportunity to understand that when people do something that hurts others, they themselves are bound by fear and delusion. Rather than rehashing events in our mind and repeatedly aiming the arrow of blame at our chosen target, we too can consciously decide to turn our minds toward something bigger. Instead of investing in fixation, we can engender the discipline to contemplate compassion.

Not blaming gives us a way to access our natural intelligence. This process takes mindfulness, awareness, discernment, and discipline, because we are going against the grain of habitual pattern. Instead of blaming, we decide to extend compassion—if only to ourselves for being trapped by a klesha like blame. When we can do this on the spot, we're no longer so predictable. The person who is expecting us to blame him might be taken aback; others might even think we are stupid or crazy. We're not stupid—in fact, we're wise. Before we were confined to a prison cell—now we are sitting on a throne in a beautiful palace.

In opening our heart, we are tapping windhorse, which

fuels the lion's delight. We begin to appreciate the peculiarities of life. We become more imaginative, able to find creative ways to uproot our own negativity by contemplating the suffering of ourselves and others. When we want to pin the blame on somebody—even ourselves—the most creative thing we can do is wish that person happiness instead. Our training is liberating us from the occupation of finger-pointing. By changing our attitude, we are moving in the direction of a future that includes joy and freedom.

12

Letting Love Flow

With wisdom in love, we can frolic in the high-lands of our natural joy.

O N THE PATH of the lion, we begin to experience moments of bliss that feel just like being in love. We feel blissful because discipline and delight are turning our mind outward. We are beginning to unravel the knot of self-obsession. Eventually, generating love becomes effortless, like the sun radiating warmth and brilliance. The sun doesn't say, "Look, I'm shining!" It is thoroughly engaged in providing for the welfare of others. This is how the genuine king and queen see clearly and love without attachment. They have learned to stabilize their minds and contemplate the happiness of others.

Stabilizing our mind any time of the day or night is like taking a mineral bath. It dissolves our stress and revitalizes us. As we anchor our mind to the breath, we feel grounded, strong, and clear. Our hassles slide away, because we're connecting with a deeper stream of energy. Is this peace the ultimate happiness? No, it's just the first stage of joy. When the wind stops blowing, the world feels peaceful. Then the sun comes out, and everything warms up.

To bring about the next level of joy, we contemplate the happiness of others. Delighting in the happiness of others is the ground upon which windhorse gallops. We are expressing the energy of love, our genuine nature. We all love to be in love, because deep inside we love caring for others. Wanting someone else to be happy is like bathing in honey and milk. We don't want him to get sick. We want her to sleep well, enjoy her food, have good windhorse.

We may become confused and think that the other person is the source of our delight—that he is the pill of love and we swallow him. Love not understood becomes clinging tight. We believe that the object of our love is a permanent source of joy. We keep going back for more. We are confusing love with fixation, which brings suffering, not joy. The permanent source of joy is our love, not another person. Being in love with a particular person helps us become familiar with the joy that comes from considering the happiness of others. We think about how to make her happy—what to give her, what to say to her, what to do with her. But true love is not dependent on any one object. True love is the natural energy of our settled mind, an inexhaustible resource that we cultivate with the appreciation of the tiger and the discipline of the lion. When we experience this big kind of love, we are experiencing virtue.

At first when we love somebody, we are delighted when anything good happens to her. She gets a promotion at work, somebody compliments her on her haircut, and we're delighted. Then our love begins to sink beneath the weight of expectation, familiarity, and attachment. Our mind closes down. Negative emotions like jealousy and anger become stronger, and our love becomes weaker. We are no longer enthralled with kindness for the other. We feel competitive. Now we are engaging in nonvirtue. How can we cultivate love when we're caught in anger and jealousy?

As long as negative emotions have the power to rule us, love is like a volcano sporadically erupting from under the earth. The lava of love bubbles up, but with attachment it cools and becomes a gray mountain. Jealousy and anger suppress and calcify our love. We don't know when it will bubble up again. We are meant not to wait for moments of love to randomly arise but to be always cultivating love like a garden. We need to till the soil so that the seed of our love can open, sprout, and break through. If we water it and give it air and sunshine, it will grow.

One way to practice the contemplation of love is to bring forth the thought "May my friend get whatever he wants." Sometimes our mind gets discursive and thinks, "Well, she shouldn't get too much ice cream; otherwise she'll get fat." Or "He doesn't need a new car—it would just go to his head." But this practice is not about preventing weight gain or vanity in those who are its object. The reason we do it is to develop the discipline to be loving and kind, even when reality isn't matching our expectations. Perhaps we feel unappreciated or belittled. We begin to harbor ill feelings for our friend because we feel ignored. We don't want her to be successful. We're afraid that if he finds a better job, we won't be good enough for him anymore. Our windhorse fizzles, and of course our friend is less attracted to us. Holding back out of jealousy, competition, or pride only makes us miserable. The struggle for control makes us prisoners of our own war.

Often people resist this contemplation on loving others because they think it's a burden. To them I say, "I'm asking you to be in love for ten minutes a day. Don't you want to be in love?" We're always contemplating something—what to wear, who to call, or how to get our way. Whatever we choose to contemplate, that's what we're going to sit in. Mulling over what someone said to us and plotting our revenge, thinking about how our spouse keeps cutting us off in conversation and wishing for her to falter, replaying an accident that already happened—this is like stewing in a toxic bath. Do we want to bathe in motor oil, or do we want to bathe in milk and honey?

When we practice being in love, we are digging deeper into our jar of virtue. We are freeing our minds from "me" and plumbing the depths of our being. Contemplating love gives us the biggest of minds. The farther our love extends, the bigger our heart grows. We can be in love with the whole world. Being in love with the whole world isn't a burden. It is great joy, the confidence of the lion.

If we lack the discipline to infuse our love with wisdom,

love can bring us down because we become attached to what we love. Then we become possessive, and we get ourselves in trouble. We encase each other with rules—we can't do this and we can't do that. We're not allowing enough openness. Wisdom understands that we all need space. Ignorance looks at another without really examining, and is fooled into thinking that this is "my" friend.

When we don't allow space, we sink into jealousy and greed, feeding our own needs. Instead of extending ourselves, we take from others and provide no space. When we have taken everything we can from one relationship, we move along to find another. We can never get enough. This is how a pauper acts. True nobility serves its own needs by serving the needs of others.

Most relationships don't work out because there's a lack of oxygen. When we first fall in love, even when we kiss, we are giving space, because we're open and curious about each other. There's no sense of ownership. As the relationship evolves, there is less and less space. Our concepts about each other begin to fill it with expectation and attachment. Love needs space. Space says, "Don't be jealous. Don't try to possess the ones you love." Love mixed with space is called letting go.

To counteract attachment, we can contemplate the space between others and ourselves. The people we love have their own breath, their own bodies, their own minds. They do not belong to us. A deeper contemplation lets wisdom penetrate even further. We can ask ourselves, "Who are my loved ones, really?" They are conglomerations of flesh and bone, thoughts and words, but they are not as solid or everlasting as we believe.

When a relationship ends, we are stricken with grief, because we are being forced to deal with space in an untimely fashion. We are reeling from our own misunderstanding. That person didn't exist the way we thought. All that remains is memories and emotions. Perhaps we mistook him for part of our own identity. He is gone, but he was never really there the way we imagined. The reality is just more blatant now. When later we say, "I'm over that; I've let go of him," what we are really saying is, "I've let go of the concept of that person and how things would be between us." Wisdom teaches us to see the space between the lines. Things aren't as solid as they appear. It was the concept that was causing us heartache.

When we let this wisdom penetrate us, we gain tremendous space because we are no longer quite so possessed by our own projections. The people we love feel less oppressed by our fixation, and genuine love has room to bloom. Using the lion's discipline, we are cultivating certainty in the bigness of our hearts instead of expecting others to cater to our small-minded needs. With wisdom in love, we can frolic in the highlands of our natural joy.

13

Generating Compassion

Radiating from basic goodness like the sun, compassion lifts us above self-involvement and brings us out of the dark age.

COMPASSION IS the unfettered yearning that responds to the world with noble heart, the understanding that others are just like us. The lion looks at the world and sees that everyone—an ant scampering along the ground, a worm crawling under the earth, a bird flying high above, an antelope darting across the plains—is motivated by desire for happiness. Everyone wants to stop suffering. From the moment we wake up until we go to bed—whether we are taking a shower, having breakfast, going to work, or watching a movie—we are all engaged in this pursuit. We spend every day hoping not to suffer. With the discipline of the lion, we actively extend that wish to others as well. This is the source of the lion's delight.

Wishing for others not to suffer may seem as futile as placing a flower down the barrel of a rifle, but the ancients say that compassion is more powerful than the anger behind the gun. Ultimately we are here because of compassion. Out of the compassion of our parents, we were fed and clothed. Someone didn't want us to be hungry or cold. The food we eat, the house in which we live, the clothing on our backs— all of it comes from compassion. It is true that there is profit involved, but mixed in with it is compassion.

Compassion is the foil of bewilderment. We all want happiness, and most of us are bewildered about how to get it. We take self-involvement as the way to achieve it. If we're always conducting ourselves like miserly business owners, thinking only of our own profit, we're only harming ourselves and others, because we are full of self-interest. Living life in this bewildered way results in pain, stress, disappointment, and regret—the fruits of nonvirtue. The Tibetan word for "self" connotes being full and falling. Being full of self-involvement immediately produces negative emotions, and that's what keeps us falling into the dark age.

Compassion, by contrast, is the mind's genuine energy, radiating from basic goodness like the sun. It lifts us above self-involvement and brings us out of the dark age. Just like the sun behind a cloud, it shines through our self-centeredness. We're rushing for the bus, but seeing another person with heavy bags slows us down. We would like her pain to stop. Compassion cuts through our speed, and we help that other person.

Compassion is based on seeing suffering, relating with it,

and letting it go. We think about the whole world and all the beings caught in tremendous suffering, and we rouse the aspiration to develop the power to ease their pain. The experience of pain brings a sense of feeling trapped, of having no way out. Contemplating that aspect of pain engenders compassion, the big heart of the lion. We wish that all beings were liberated into the light of their own wisdom and compassion, so they would no longer suffer.

To contemplate compassion, we first bring to mind a personal experience that evokes it. Sitting there and thinking, "May everyone not suffer" can be too vague; such a big thought—in the beginning, at least—might not give rise to much compassion. I often begin by remembering the time I saw a dog being hit by a car. The car screeched to a halt, the dog whimpered and cried. It was hit in the hindquarters; its legs were dragging. Without thought, my heart jumped out with a strong desire for its pain to stop. Bringing to mind that personal experience always arouses a feeling of compassion in me. That's how we make compassion powerful—by kindling its spark on an intimate level. The Buddha taught that we can have that intimate feeling of compassion for all sentient beings.

When the feeling of compassion arises, we meditate on our response for a moment, and compassion begins to flow. Now that we've generated compassion, we can extend it to our family and friends, little by little. This is how we make it bigger. If we bring intelligence into our compassion, we can extend it even to our enemy. People are always being pushed around by their own anger and pride. When we're in an adversarial relationship with someone, if we can see that his suffering arises from the negative emotion that is torturing him—like a victim and his bully—we can feel compassion.

Compassion even has the power to overcome demons—invisible beings who are trapped in negative emotions and wrong views. Caught between lives, they harm others out of ignorance. There are stories of Tibetan Buddhist lamas trying to banish demons with exorcisms and spells, to no avail. But when the lamas extended compassion to them, the demons found peace and were liberated from their painful state.

There are two kinds of compassion: compassion mixed with clinging and compassion mixed with prajna—best knowledge. The compassion we feel toward friends and family is usually mixed with clinging. We want the best for them, but our wish is colored by jealousy, attachment, or fear. Clinging makes it hard to be straightforward in our compassion. We're still thinking of ourselves. We want someone's suffering to go away because it is inconvenient for us, it scares us, or it causes us personal pain. Through contemplative meditation, we filter out the dirt of negative emotions and hit the mother lode of virtue—unadulterated, openhearted compassion.

The Buddha said, "Don't just take my word for it, contemplate it. It's better for you to convince yourself than for me to convince you." Convincing ourselves is practice. In contemplation, we practice pointing ourselves in a particular direction and staying there for a while. When we hold our mind to something, it has no alternative but to get more familiar with that place. That's the meaning of one Tibetan word for meditation, "familiarity." Another Tibetan word for practice means "bring it into experience." When we contemplate compassion, placing our mind on the welfare of others, we recognize and acknowledge when we are thinking of ourselves instead. Then we return our mind to the thought of compassion. This is how we become familiar with compassion and bring it into our experience.

When we experience compassion, we pan its gold with prajna, knowing how things are. With prajna's insight, we learn to extend compassion to others not because we are attached to them or afraid of their pain but because we know that all beings want happiness, just like ourselves. Just like us, they do not want pain. With this knowledge and understanding, we can extend our care to others like the warm rays of the sun that shines on the lion's highland meadow. The more compassion we generate, the bigger our mind becomes. Since compassion brings joy, it makes us happy.

When we wake up in the morning, we should remember that all lasting happiness comes from wisdom and compassion. Compassion is not simply a feeble response to overwhelming greed and aggression. The mind of wisdom and compassion is the victory banner of the golden age. When we raise this flag in our life, windhorse increases.

14

The Confidence of Delight
in Helping Others

When our attitude is open, we can have fun with
what the world presents.

ONE OF THE GREAT Indian teachers, Shantideva,
who wrote about the path of the bodhisattva-warrior,
said, "The discomfort of contemplating the welfare of others
is small compared with the benefit we get from it." Just thinking about how to help others relieves stress, brings joy to our
mind, and has fantastic karmic repercussions. This is how
the discipline of the lion enriches the world with the confidence of joy, which expresses itself as the ability to uplift any
situation with the question "How can I help?"

Most of us spend our day in a continual contemplation
about how we can help ourselves. With the lion's discipline

and delight, we learn to flip that contemplation inside out. At first, we might forget to do it. Then we might feel frustrated because we do not know how to help others. Even though people are always asking me how to do it, I can't tell you. I can only encourage you to make it a central theme in your contemplation and your activity. Contemplating how to be helpful opens our hearts and our horizons. By remembering the basic intention of a ruler—to ensure others' welfare—we are laying the ground for enriching our family or business, and ultimately for our own happiness and success.

If we have a family, we can take a few minutes in the morning to contemplate our commitment to them. We may have concerns about the mortgage, the children's schoolwork, or someone's health. Before we get all caught up in the day-to-day, we can step back and uplift our mind with this thought—"May my family be happy. May they not suffer." First we stabilize our mind by focusing it on the breath for a few minutes. Then we place our mind on this thought. When we notice that we're thinking about something else, we bring our mind back to the thought.

With this gut-level wish, we are generating the discipline and delight of the lion. We are reminding ourselves of heaven—the view on which we are going to base all the decisions we need to make. This strengthens and deepens our commitment to our family before we come down to the nitty-gritty decision making of earth. By first contemplating our view, we can learn to bring the joyful confidence of the lion into whatever the day offers. That confidence will take us beyond the fear and hesitation that keep us stuck in "me."

We may have a million thoughts about *how* we want our family to be happy—eating the right food, making a good grade, having the right clothes and friends. If we focus on those thoughts and concerns too much, we lose track of why we are nourishing our family in the first place, and we become oppressed by our lives, as if we are looking at the earth under our feet all the time, forgetting to lift our gaze to the sky. Contemplation is a way to orient our mind before the day begins. Regardless of what school our children are attending, we want them to have joy in their lives, and not to be plagued by suffering. In focusing on that intention, we are reminding ourselves that underneath all the meaningless mental drama, we possess the wish-fulfilling jewel, the enlightened mind of *bodhichitta*, the wisdom and compassion that ride on windhorse.

We may say, "I don't need to contemplate my wish for others to be happy. I already know what I'm doing." But often if we do not consciously bring to mind our motivation for others not to suffer, the wish-fulfilling jewel becomes hazy and distant. The more superficial aspects of our life take over, and we become fixated on who didn't put the milk away or who's hogging the remote. We lose touch with the deeper reason we're together. What is not foremost in the mind, we tend to forget.

That is why we contemplate how to help. We are learning to draw conclusions that will lead to stronger windhorse. The longer we hold our mind to a particular thought—"May my family be free from suffering"—the sooner we arrive at a point of truth: our genuine intention is for others to be happy, but irritation often obscures that wish. We realize that others' happiness is the root of all happiness, and that all happiness is rooted in freedom from ignorance. When our mind has become familiar with thoughts like these, those truths become the foundation of our life. This is how we transform from pauper into ruler.

If we have a business, we can start our day in the office by taking the time to remember why we are working: in order to be happy, we all need money to provide for our families and ourselves. We simply sit at our desk for five minutes, let our mind settle, and place it on the thought "May my co-workers be happy." Some people might not be working as hard as they should; some people may have made mistakes. These local ups and downs will always be with us, so we needn't become overly distracted by them. We can settle to a deeper level of consciousness. Orienting our mind toward heaven helps us be magnanimous, as opposed to oppressive. Throughout the workday, we can contemplate the thought "May I offer myself as a vehicle for others' happiness."

Once we're inspired to uplift our mind and look out for the welfare of others, we can always find a way to help. The discipline of the lion is the starting place, because it lifts us above doubt and laziness. We can practice speaking encouraging words, even when we're feeling speedy or depressed. We can make time to help our child with homework or cook an omelet for a friend. Helping others is not about specifics—"Should I make a Spanish omelet or a cheese omelet?" The point is to generate a sense of warmth and openness while we are doing it, cultivating delight that we are able to help.

As far as the details go, when our attitude is open, we can have fun with what the world presents. Instead of feeling angry that there's no cheese in the fridge, or that we have run out of eggs, we can use whatever happens to uplift the moment. We can play with the whole situation—enjoy making a casserole instead of an omelet, or go to the store in the spirit of helping. The discipline of not resisting circumstances is how we drop our concepts and move forward, bringing everything that happens to the point of our contemplation.

Opening our heart is like tilling a new garden. At first it's rough, because the soil needs working and there are plenty of rocks to remove. We feel discouraged. We're so accustomed to putting ourselves first that thinking of others may seem impersonal and arduous. But over time the soil softens up, and our heart naturally begins to sprout kindness, compassion, and joy. The more we help others, the softer and more fertile our heart becomes.

Helping others represents a new approach to life. We don't check it off our list and then go back to "What about me?" Feeling puffed up about helping, as if it's an important new project, is not confidence; it's a sign that we're using our practice to fortify small-mindedness. We think we're better than others; they're privileged that we're helping them. If we act out of pity or duty rather than care and warmth, making someone else the most elaborate meal will not bring us joy.

Instead, we'll feel tired, because we're not really thinking of others, we're thinking of ourselves. We'll often draw a blank about how to help, because our caring energy isn't flowing outward yet. We don't really know how to give. We might be tempted to give up and forget about helping others. Then we're not helping ourselves, either.

We may be sitting there contemplating others, and in the back of our mind thinking, "I need to do more for myself." By thinking of others, we *are* doing more for ourselves. Generating joy by helping others is a secret way—and the best way—of helping ourselves. Every time we think of someone else's happiness, we are taking a vacation from the "me" plan. It's like getting physically fit by helping our neighbor shovel the snow from her driveway.

At first we continue to think of ourselves because that's our habit. We're also not quite convinced that thinking of others is worth it. We shouldn't feel bad if we think, "If I help them, maybe they'll help me." Even if we're stuck on helping others as a way of helping ourselves, instead of having a hundred thoughts about "me," we might have at least thirty about others. Over time, as we stay with the discipline of helping others, the ratio will shift and the joy of the lion will percolate our self-absorption. We'll have more thoughts about others, fewer about ourselves. We're getting used to our new way of life, and we can see that it's working. Little by little, our windhorse is rising, because we're using our day as a way to practice virtue. As in all contemplations, we are starting in a small place to get to a big one.

When my mother was ill, I watched as Lama Pegyal, an accomplished meditation practitioner, helped her. He would talk to her softly, bring her water, and gently turn her over in bed when she was sore. Every move he made demonstrated genuine kindness rooted simply in wanting my mother not to be in pain. I realized that all of us can embody that kind of generosity throughout the day. We can bring someone a cup of coffee, let our friend read the newspaper in silence, give our spouse another napkin when hers has fallen on the floor. We can help push the car when it's stuck in the snow. Even though these acts of kindness may be unappreciated or unseen, we should keep our practice up. The sun shines, whether it is day or night, and so should our concern for others.

Enriching our thoughts and actions with love and compassion releases tremendous positive energy, as if our windhorse has been liberated. Like churning milk into butter, there is alchemy involved. When we churn "What about me?" into "What about you?" we are consciously changing our molecular structure by engaging the big-mind chromosome. The result is ziji—radiant inner confidence. As we turn our energy outward, we are present for the world in the wholehearted manner of a child offering a gift. There are no politics involved, no scheming, no manipulation. Our compassion beams outward in delight at the happiness of others.

IV

THE PATH
OF THE GARUDA

15

The Truth about Existence

The mind of the garuda is outrageous because it is
no longer on the "me" plan.

I RECENTLY REACHED AGE FORTY, a turning point in
most people's lives. Before that birthday, people would
routinely describe me as a "young lama" or a "young teacher."
They were always exclaiming, "You're so young!" But when I
turned forty, something surprising happened. They started
saying, "Oh, you're getting old." One day I was young, and the
next day I was old. One day I had all the time in the world,
and the next, time was running out. I thought, "What happened to the in-between period when I could just be an ordinary adult?"

Tibetans are cheerful about getting older, because they
are proud to have lived another year. People in the West seem
to take a different attitude. We sometimes have a hard time

accepting change, especially when it involves aging, sickness, and death. We feel depressed about getting older, because we are getting further from being young. I certainly don't mind getting older. I've enjoyed the process of growing and learning. I owe my appreciation in part to my teachers, who taught me to contemplate the truths of human existence. They would often laugh as they talked about all the different ways we could die. They said, "Ultimately, death comes without warning." They were not being callous or vindictive. They knew the power that comes from contemplating reality. It frees our mind from hope and fear. Now I know that I can either fight impermanence tooth and nail or accept it and grow from there.

We start aging as soon as we are born. Birth is both a delightful and a painful experience. As children, we all have growing pains connected with being fascinated by and fearful of the world. As teenagers, we give birth to incredible intelligence and skepticism, but we have little experience. As adults, we experience the stress and pain that come with knowledge and responsibility, and eventually the aging, sickness, and suffering associated with death.

Often older people say, "I wish I'd known what I know now when I was young." By contemplating the truth about existence, we *can* know it while we're young. If we accept impermanence, we can dare to live beyond hope and fear of what will happen next. This is the outrageousness of the garuda, a mythical bird with human arms that hatches from space fully developed. The garuda is outrageous not because it jumps up and down in attention-getting ways but because it has abandoned the reference point of "me." It has total perspective, a fresh mind that cuts through concept with a "self-existing sword," as one Shambhala text says. Therefore the mind of the garuda knows no boundaries. This is truly outrageous. The garuda knows that sickness, aging, and death are teachings, if we can accept them. A separation, a death, a birth, an illness is like a drop of water. We can be drowned by it or nourished by it.

Sometimes just watching people step off a bus, I think, "Everybody is going through a crisis—a midlife crisis, an adolescent crisis, a senior crisis. The young are worried about education so they can get a job. The middle-aged are concerned about working hard so they can afford retirement. The old people are worried about being lonely and not burdening their children. Others are just having a life crisis. They're afraid of life, or they think they're missing something." We become self-obsessed and down on ourselves because we can't accept our suffering.

Change causes anxiety and suffering. That suffering doesn't have to be personal, as though we're being singled out, but most of us do take it personally. When what we want doesn't happen, we think we've lost; when it does, we think we've won. When our car is stolen, when we get sick, when we lose our job or have to move, we feel baffled, surprised, or insulted. We want the pain to go away. When we win at poker, finish a project, or fall in love, we feel elated, confirmed, or on top of the world. We want our pleasure to last as long as possible.

Contemplating the truth about existence reveals that life

is constant change. The Buddha says, "You may be in a good situation, but it won't last. Everything you see is impermanent. Everybody experiences birth, aging, sickness, death." We think, "He seems to be right about that. All the people I know will pass away; everything in this material world will dissolve."

When I went to Nalanda University in India—for centuries the epicenter of Buddhist learning—I was greeted by a few dilapidated structures. Of the Greek and Roman empires and the Asian empire of Kublai Khan, all that remain are some names, some stories, and a few ruins. If that is what happens to the greatest earthly achievements, what hope do we have of creating anything permanent?

Contemplating worldly gain and loss reveals that we spend part of our life trying to get it together, and the other part watching it fall apart. As soon as we have time—"I have a whole hour free"—we are losing it. As soon as we make a friend, we're losing him. As soon as we have fame, it becomes tinged with notoriety. As soon as we have wealth, we're losing it. Looking for something new to gain helps us forget to look but a few seconds back at the last thing that we lost. Fabricating this chain of desire is how we keep ourselves in samsara. We are using instability to try to make stability. We're investing in hope and fear, banking on denial of a simple truth: all the pleasure the world can offer eventually turns to pain. Everything we gain is subject to loss.

Why do we put all that effort into gain when, in the end, we are going to lose it? Has anything we've gained brought us lasting happiness? Is there anything we own that we will be able to keep? What in our lives is not subject to the winds of gain and loss? Even this body will dissolve. In the face of death, there is only basic goodness. Gain and loss is just an illusion—one that we've allowed to rule us.

Contemplating the truth about existence invites us to let go of our attachment to hope that we will gain something and fear that we will lose it. It gives us the perspective to see that life is constantly happening to us, and that's okay. What causes suffering is our desire for things to be a certain way. Most of us wake up in the morning with a faulty assumption that we are going to get happiness by dividing our day into what we want to happen and what we don't want to happen, into those who are for us and those who are against us. The mind of the garuda reveals hope and fear for what they are—simple fabrications of the mind, like random spots we mark on the tablet of the sky. If change walks into that space, we feel threatened, because we've frozen it with an idea of how we want the world to be. The world we build with our illusory expectations is that absurd. We need to change our attitude.

The garuda flies high in the sky, looking at the ups and downs of life with a bird's-eye view. We are seeing clearly and flying free because we've cut through the web of opinions, desires, and avoidance tactics that keep us bound to "me." We see how measuring our lives with this unstable standard makes us paupers. It shrinks our vision and dulls our sword of wisdom. How can we stay in the present moment when we're ruled by hope and fear of what might happen next?

Contemplating impermanence results in a mind that says, "Bracing myself against the truth is not going to make it disappear. Worrying about sickness and death is not going to improve my health or make dying any less eventual." When we've contemplated reality face-to-face, we're more cheerful in any situation. We no longer waste time feeling sorry for ourselves. We're not afraid of change. We can act in the most outrageous way: to free ourselves from the conventional mind that is fixated on how we want the world to be, attached to hope that it will meet our expectation and fear that it will not.

From its first leap into space, the garuda can fly anywhere, because its wings are balanced, neither buoyed up by hope nor weighed down by fear. Knowing that there is nothing to possess but our own awareness gives us the freedom to dwell in that space. With the big mind of the garuda, we have an intelligence that balances our life. On the one hand, when we miss the plane because of a traffic jam, we don't become upset, because our mind is big enough to see it as a passing inconvenience. On the other hand, when someone gives us thousands of air miles so that we can take a vacation, we don't become elated, as if our suffering is permanently resolved.

This kind of outrageousness in the face of change takes practice. Letting go of thoughts as we watch them rise and fall in meditation, we've become familiar with the space beyond our discursiveness. With practice, that space gets bigger—so big that it can accommodate whatever our day presents. When we feel disappointed or excited, we can regain our balance by taking a deep breath, looking up at the sky, or even smiling as we dissolve our attachment to how we think things ought to be. We're not playing Pollyanna, we're learning to let go and fly in the space of things as they are. Meditation has shown us that our mind is not solid. It is not made of earth. We cannot measure basic goodness. What brings measure to mind is expectation—hope and fear. Knowing the reality of change, we accept gain and loss—no hope and fear attached. When we do this, we become naturally and spontaneously lighthearted. We are no longer trying to cure change by applying fixation. Rather, we accept what the moment presents and use it to expand our heart and mind.

I was recently looking at a magazine article called "Ten Things to Do Before You Die." I have a list of one. Before we die, we should all experience our wisdom and compassion. If we don't experience that, the list of ten things will grow to a hundred or a thousand. As if our mind has a tapeworm, we will constantly be consuming, never satisfied, always looking for the thing that will finally "do it" for us. That hungry feeling is doubt—doubt of basic goodness. Doubt is not recognizing the glory of our own being. We don't see that basic goodness is everywhere. When we have confidence in our true nature, we can glide in the sky of our impartial mind, no matter what changes on the outside. True victory is not being caught by the illusion of permanence. This freedom allows us to extend ourselves outrageously, with wisdom and compassion, in all worlds.

16

The Virtue of Letting Go

Without attachment to the myth of "me," we are much happier.

I F WE TAKE A CAREFUL LOOK at hope and fear, underneath all of it we find attachment. We might think that to overcome attachment we have to get rid of whatever it is we're clinging to—our favorite sweater, our relationship, or the ice cream we love to eat. We think, "I am so fixated on ice cream, I need to give it up. I see myself pushing other people out of the way so I can get to the counter first." But the problem isn't the ice cream. The problem isn't even that we're pushing people. The problem is our view. We want things to be a certain way, and we push in that direction. The garuda knows that there is nothing to get. The only thing we own is our attachment, and attachment creates karma. This is how wanting puts our world in motion.

Knowing that attachment creates karma is relative

prajna—best knowledge. Developing prajna takes constant reflection. There are three kinds of prajna: hearing about the truth, contemplating the truth, then meditating and becoming familiar with the truth directly in our immediate experience. The Buddha says, "The world is fluid, not solid. It's fixating on what you want that hurts. Stop clinging so tightly." We hear this and it strikes a chord. Could it be true? We contemplate it, we chew on it; we mull it over. We look at our behavior. What the Buddha said begins to make sense. The world is moving, and it hurts when our mind tries to stop it. Letting go begins to seem like a good idea. We should stop clinging so tightly. How do we do this? We meditate. In meditation, we become familiar with letting go. We watch our thoughts arise and let them go. We're spreading our wings, loosening up, so that we can let go anytime. The flexibility of the garuda is the cause and result of letting go.

When we rise from our meditation seat, we can continue the practice of letting go as we bring it forth into our day. When we're about to sink into a depression or indulge in discursiveness, we can remember that letting go is an endless possibility, one that lets us soar into our life instead of being oppressed by it. This process takes coaxing. It's like dealing with two children fighting over a toy. If we convince one of the children that she doesn't need that toy, after a while she gives birth to a little prajna and lets go. She may immediately turn around and grab something else, but that moment of letting go, of emptiness, is prajna. The child is no longer angry or possessive.

Such moments help us realize that clinging will never

lead to lasting happiness. For example, feeling love for the people and things around us might create a sense of attachment. We want to possess what we love. Prajna helps us see that our attachment isn't even to that person or that thing; we are just attached to being attached. We're having a knee-jerk reaction. We may not be angry with someone in particular—we're just angry. Our anger finds a target, and we fixate. The virtue of the garuda is letting go.

Letting go of attachment is the ultimate generosity, because it connects us with our wisdom and compassion. It can be as simple as shutting your mouth instead of yelling at somebody, or turning off the television, walking to your meditation seat, and working with your mind. It is getting up early to contemplate compassion, even though you'd like more sleep. Letting go is thinking of the comfort of others before your own. It's coming in from the cold and making someone else a hot drink before you make one for yourself. It's saying "I love you" when you're afraid the other person doesn't feel the same. It's saying "I'm sorry" when you think the other person is to blame.

Sometimes letting go is keeping things to yourself. When I ran my first marathon, everything was going well. Then at about mile six, I felt a blister developing on my right foot. In putting on a pair of new socks that morning, I had violated a cardinal rule: never use new equipment on race day. What was I to do? Changing my stride would affect my time. I had to be sensible—but how sensible is running 26.2 miles? I decided to run on the blister so it would pop. The pain became a meditation of sorts, and after a while, I let it go. I finished the race in decent time. The friends I was running with were surprised I hadn't mentioned the blister, which was now quite bloody. But if I had told them about it, they would only have worried, and there was nothing to be done. It was better to let go.

We often find it difficult to let go, because the modern world is so competitive. Competition doesn't enable us to accomplish what we want. It just introduces the hook of trying to gain by outdoing somebody else. We are as good as we are, and forcing another person down doesn't make us any better. Trying to manipulate the environment by promoting ourselves and hoping for others to fail is cowardly, not outrageous. When the winner of a sports competition is asked what she did to win, the reply often points to an inner balance and relaxation that enabled her to perform well, rarely to a desperation that drove her to beat somebody else. Many world-record holders say that when they ran the hundred meters or did the long jump, it felt effortless. That balance is windhorse, a selfless synchronization that comes from letting go.

What do we discover when we let go? Space. Sometimes it is known as openness, selflessness, or emptiness. Is it empty because we lost something? No, it is empty of our concept of what we thought it was. Emptiness is empty of our assumptions, and it is full of compassion. This is basic goodness. Discovering it is freedom. We realize that assumptions are the basis of most of our experiences. We discover that when the mind and the world are empty of those assumptions, we can live in space like the garuda because we're running on equanimity instead of attachment.

If we keep letting go, at some point prajna will reveal that there was never really anything to hold on to. Life at the core is radiant wisdom and compassion. It is empty and liberated from the idea of having to be a thing or have a thing. Prajna leads to fearlessness, because it gives us perspective on our suffering. We're more patient, no longer so dependent on things going our way. Without attachment to the myth of "me," we are much happier. We feel clean, more available to others. It's like when we have told the truth—our mind feels crisp and clear. Our body feels more confident. Now we can leap into space and soar, because we're riding on windhorse instead of on attachment.

17

The Confidence of Equanimity

When we have gone beyond the boundaries of hope and fear, we are able to work with whatever comes our way.

THE GARUDA'S outrageousness doesn't mean that we act recklessly out of frustration, impatience, or boredom. It is confidence full-fledged. When we have gone beyond the boundaries of hope and fear, we are able to work with whatever comes our way. Our judgment is exact, according to the situation. Though leaving "me" behind does not protect us from misfortune, it takes us beyond our concepts to a place where few dare go. This kind of outrageousness brings exuberance in a surprising form—equanimity. Equanimity is a balanced state of mind. With equanimity we can glide evenly through our day, because we no longer get hooked by negative emotion.

One summer when I was teaching at Shambhala Mountain Center in Colorado, we had an incredible heat wave. In the midst of it, my uncle Damchö Rinpoche, my cousin Karma Sengay Rinpoche, and two monks arrived on their first trip out of Tibet. Day and night they wore the same heavy clothes, the Tibetan equivalent of a woolen suit. At one point I asked Damchö Rinpoche, "Don't you feel hot?" He answered, "Well, apart from the feeling of heat, I am okay." I understood him to be saying, "There's this feeling, and I could be attached to it, or I could not be attached to it. If I were attached to it, then how would my life be? I would be taking off clothes and putting on clothes all day long, spending most of my time trying to get comfortable. Instead, I could just sit here and enjoy what is happening." So that was what he was doing. People are always saying, "I'm happy to be here," but he really meant it. That is equanimity.

Equanimity is the mind's natural joy. It comes from cultivating wisdom and compassion. When we are strong enough to extend our love toward everyone, without bias, we enter the garuda mind. This might happen for only moments at a time, but that's okay. Because I meet with others constantly, I am always watching people struggle with their minds. Do we have to keep things churning in order to feel alive? Having equanimity means we've given it a break. We've relaxed our mind; the brilliance of the Rigden is present and engaged.

The garuda knows that wherever we are, no matter what we are doing, we can feel the awareness of the Rigden—

basic goodness, beginninglessness, and endless freedom. Our basic goodness is not created by hope coming true, nor is it deflated when fear raises its head. It does not depend on externals. It doesn't wax or wane from one moment to the next. With this impartial mind, we can practice compassion and wisdom freely.

Without equanimity, we might be able to feel some compassion, but it would be only for those we care about or those who arouse it easily. With that limited form of compassion, we will also develop aggression, because we don't want anyone to harm those we care about. We're still believing in the dead world, which is conditioned by hope and fear. With a static point of view, we imagine that the world came from somewhere, that it is going somewhere, and that there is something to be gained or lost. Equanimity liberates our attachment so that we can accept the world as it is—constantly changing and alive with basic goodness.

Sometimes we think that, because we are in modern times, we have modern views. No matter what the era, however, there will always be some variation of two basic views, reflections of hope and fear. The first view is eternalism. Eternalism has it that a permanent, unchanging creator made the earth. People with this view believe that their actions influence this life and what happens afterward, but they think there is a supervisor who remains unchanging.

The second view is nihilism. In ancient India there was a school called Jangpenpa. Its followers did not believe in karma. They believed that you have only one life to live, and you might as well live it the best you can. The only criterion for this life was how much fun you could have. Whoever had the best time had the best life. There was no previous life, no previous karma. At the time of death, the elements of the body would separate and the consciousness would just dissolve into space. There would be no afterlife. If you had a good time, you did a good job. If you didn't—too bad, because you wouldn't be getting another chance.

Another view is the view of the Buddha, who looked at things from a relative and absolute perspective. This view is called the middle way. People often mistakenly think that *middle* refers to the way between the two extremes of eternalism and nihilism, between existence and nonexistence. But *middle* refers to the fact that this approach surpasses existence or nonexistence. It is a balanced view.

According to this view, things exist on a relative level—we have a name and an address, and the car we drive takes us to a restaurant. The objects of our sense perceptions—sight, sound, smell, taste, and touch—appear, but they are not inherently permanent. On an ultimate level, they are as ephemeral as last night's dream. They are beyond the hope and fear of eternalism and nihilism, beyond the concepts of real or not real, existing or not existing. It's like talking about what happened yesterday. Today, whatever happened yesterday is beyond what we think happened or did not happen.

Uma, the middle way, is known as freedom. It is free from the *concept* of existence and nonexistence—both and neither. What sees the freedom beyond these four extremes? The wisdom of prajna. Prajna is called "best knowledge" because it takes us toward experiencing reality directly, without the veil of "me." The garuda's equanimity gives birth to deeper prajna. The projections we create with fixed mind seem thinner as the sword of prajna makes a little tear in the fabric of illusion. Eventually, we move beyond perceiving things in a dualistic way. This experience is known as emptiness. It is empty of concept and duality. The garuda hatches full-blown and able to fly because it is not afraid to leap into the open space of the present moment. It can soar above attachment to its own projections, into the sky of impartial mind.

When we think of living without attachment, we might imagine someone like Mahatma Gandhi, or a yogi living in a cave. But the Buddha taught that there are two worldly lifestyles that exemplify the equanimity of the garuda—that of the enlightened ascetic and that of the enlightened ruler. Since both have renounced attachment, one is no better than the other. Both are benefiting others, but in different ways. For example, the Buddha was the total ruler of his world, even though he abandoned material possessions. The first king of Shambhala, Dawa Sangpo, was totally enlightened, even though he lived in a palace. Nonattachment is a view, not a vocation. It comes from seeing the illusory quality of ourselves and our experiences.

As Shambhala kings and queens, we embody basic goodness: profound, brilliant, just, powerful, and all-victorious. Abandoning attachment to "me," we use our presence in the world to reflect that confidence: we dress well, eat well, think well, and live well because we respect our dignity as truly human beings who can cultivate ziji—inner confidence—to bring about windhorse, success that includes peace, happiness, and material prosperity. Our strength does not come from outer wealth, however; it comes from knowing that there is nothing to be given or taken away. The equanimity of the garuda has become a personal field of power.

In Tibet, this field of power is wangthang. *Wang* means "power," and *thang* means "expanse." Wangthang is authentic presence that arises from true wealth, the realization of emptiness and compassion. Free from fixed mind, we are liberated into the magic of things as they are. We see that others have fixed mind and therefore experience suffering. We realize in an outrageous moment that if we approach all beings with kindness, appreciation, and love, we can be happy anytime, anywhere. Our love is liberated from the prison of bias. We are like the garuda; the world does not impinge on our freedom. With this field of power, we magnetize whatever we need to move forward. We are gathering the drala of richness. The world is continuously rich; whether we seemingly gain or lose something does not matter.

Equanimity is confidence that is free from attachment. It takes practice, especially when we are still being fooled by the highs and lows of samsara. The best way to cultivate equanimity is to bring our mind back to the fluid nature of ourselves and the world, the dreamlike quality of appearances. Everything is changing all the time. Our longing for our friend can change from love to anger in an instant. What we think will make us happy shifts from moment to moment. What will happen tomorrow is happening only in our mind today, along with what happened yesterday.

When it sees that the mind is not solid, the garuda sees that the world is not solid, either. Inherently, all is emptiness and compassion. When we see the world this way, we're not so obsessed with duality. Now we can follow the garuda's example—take a leap into space. Do something outrageous. Accept whatever happens as the self-existing wisdom of things as they are, and use it to nurture wisdom and compassion.

Outrageousness can be smiling at the person sitting next to us on the subway, not making such fixed plans all the time, or realizing that our life—and the meaning of our life—is made not just of how many things went right and wrong for us. Since others around us may live their lives in hope and fear, it takes courage to leap, and we can't be idiotic about our leaping. For example, deciding to quit one's job without knowing what's going to happen next is not necessarily outrageous. Knowing when it's time to quit and doing it could be.

With the garuda in our life, we have total perspective, even under the most challenging circumstances. We know the truth about existence, the flower of compassion is blooming, and ziji—brilliant confidence—is giving us a field of power in which to spread our wings. We start to glow, which magnetizes whatever we need to fuel windhorse—the confidence in basic goodness that brings true success and happiness.

V

THE PATH
OF THE DRAGON

18

The Virtue of Knowing Selflessness

Losing the idea of "me" is the point of liberation.

WHEN MY FRIEND Jon and I were running in the Scottish Highlands one day, we came into a valley and saw a big dog. We started strategizing how we were going to avoid being attacked. Should we run? We were already running. What about climbing a tree? There wasn't a tree in sight. As we approached the "dog," we realized it was just a large stone. We laughed at ourselves and kept running. We had created an object in our minds and then responded to it with fear. We were afraid of our projection, which had stemmed from ignorance. The minute we saw our mistake, the fear dissolved. Our relief came from seeing how things really were. Seeing things as they are is prajna, the self-existing confidence of the dragon.

The dragon is a symbol of rulers and master meditators.

It represents ultimate wisdom, confidence, and power. There is something inscrutable about the dragon, something that cannot be understood. It has the form of a serpent, yet it flies. There are many stories about dragons, but who has seen one? The Tibetan word for thunder is *drukdra*—the sound of dragons. Like thunder, the wisdom of the dragon wakes us up. It shatters conceptual mind and uproots our insecurity.

The dragon says, "I dance and play in the depth of your own mind. Let me out!" The dragon mind is fathomless. It cannot be read. It rests naturally in the Great Eastern Sun—the wisdom of prajna. With prajna, our mind goes beyond the limits of space. The Shambhala teachings describe the dragon mind as "space which cannot be punctured by an arrow." The dragon is deep wisdom that looks precisely at everything. It sees how we're always trying to make appearances into "things," projecting a concrete world onto a fluid process. We say, "I have a self. I exist," but there is no self in the way we perceive the self. Just as I mistook a rock for a dog, we are always mistaking our ever-changing experience for a solid self or "me." As we continue to sit quietly, meditating and contemplating, we begin to understand that our own wisdom is always trying to awaken us to this truth, which is as elusive as the breath, or as the dragon itself.

We can start by contemplating what the Buddha said: the self we imagine to be solid and continuous is really just a gathering of ingredients—heaps. It is the conjunction of blood, bones, memories, emotions, thoughts, and perceptions. When we experience this conglomeration of elements, ignorance says, "I think I'll call this 'me.' " We are creating an illusion and giving it a name. Not only is the illusion transparent and dreamlike but the things we make it with are the same. It's like watching clouds form into the shape of a dragon. We know it's not a dragon. We know the clouds themselves are not really solid. But when we see that form, we give it a name—something recognizable.

The moment we mistake the collection of heaps for "me," attachment arises, fear arises, pride arises—and we believe in "me." This projection forces us to perceive the whole world in a certain way. We think, "I'm real, and so are they," and therefore it follows, "If I'm real and they take something away, I will get mad." We suffer from that ignorance. Suffering is the reverberation of not knowing selflessness, the virtue of the dragon.

In his first teaching after his enlightenment, the Buddha made this very point. Life is painful for the basic reason that we are self-obsessed. Sometimes we think, "If I didn't feel angry and jealous, then I would have peace." In fact, negative emotions are simply the embodiment of thinking of a self. Every time we feel irritation or attachment, we are experiencing self-absorption.

If we contemplate this, we will see that it's true. Anger, desire, jealousy—all negative emotions are rooted in attachment to "me." They are fighting a losing battle, for there is no "me." If there is a self, where is it? Contemplating selflessness reveals that looking for "me" is like trying to find the horizon. It looks like a straight line, and from afar it's a definite geographical reference point. But if we're asked to pinpoint it, we'll only go in circles. We'll never find it. We'll just find moods that come and go. Those moods are also selfless; they come and go because they are on unstable ground. There is not another self, apart from the self we try to hold together with the pride of our view, seeing ourselves as separate from—and maybe slightly better than—everything else. The bewilderment from which this pride arises is always telling us a lie. We're making a cloud into a mountain. Without this confusion, there is no belief in a self, for there is no self-infatuation.

Even when we speak of selflessness, the mind goes to "me." We think, "I'm selfless," but everything is selfless. Saying "everything is selfless" is like calling that stone "dogless." It might give the impression that a dog was there at some point, but it never was. It was our idea of a dog that was there. Similarly, we say that everything is selfless, but the self was never there. There was only our idea of a self. When we realize that we have always been selfless, what is missing? The conceptual mind that centralizes into "me" and then projects a world out there that is solid and separate. Who we think we are and what we think of the world is a concept that we are creating with our mind. We create a concept in our mind and we believe that concept. Our belief in a self is the most obvious example of this fundamental ignorance.

The wisdom of the dragon asks us to contemplate why we are trying to make things so solid. What is it we're trying to hold together? The chair is not saying it's a chair, nor are our arms and legs and chest saying, "I'm me." Our mind is weaving the elements of our body, feelings, sense perceptions, and judgments into a solid entity called "me." "Me" is a mental fabrication. There is no "me," and that's okay. Seeing this and losing the idea of "me" is the point of liberation. What is liberated? Lungta—windhorse—and the wish-fulfilling jewel of wisdom and compassion.

Because negative emotions are rooted in ignorance, it's sometimes hard to know when we are bound by their influence. To see them we need prajna, which grows from the mindfulness and awareness of the tiger. It is enriched by the discipline and joy of the lion. With the sharp eyes of the garuda, it recognizes when negativity has thrown us off balance. When we blame, cling, compete, or complain, prajna sees these signs of self-fabrication. It knows what we need to do when they arise: generate compassion and courage, the fortitude to overcome fear. Fear is just lack of prajna. Prajna and compassion are the ultimate drala, because they burn through negativity like a laser. The result is great bliss, a mind that has risen above the mistake of the self.

When my own teachers would ask me to look for my self, in the beginning I thought, "What a silly question. I'm right here." When I tried to figure out exactly where "here" was, it became a little tricky. I had assumed a "here." My body might be sitting in a chair right now, but where is the body I had when I was three? Where is the self I thought I was yesterday? And where is my mind? Westerners think the mind is in the head; Tibetans think it's in the heart. In looking for my mind, I discovered that it seems to be in many different places. Sometimes it is drinking a glass of water, remembering swimming in the summer, feeling the breeze. In this contemplation, I observed that the self is more elusive than I thought. Thus began my journey into discovering that my experiences are not as real and solid as I had assumed. Questioning that assumption is what my teachers wanted me to do.

My teachers then instructed me to contemplate appearances—all the things I could see, touch, smell, hear, or taste. Which of those things is not generated by mind? The conclusion I drew was that if my mind weren't here to experience these appearances and—if what they were saying is true—generate them, then I would have no way of knowing if something is not generated by the mind. My teachers wanted me to realize the power of the mind and how it generates our whole environment. We think that there is a self, and that everything else is separate from it. But there is no self, and nothing is separate from selflessness.

When I ask people to contemplate selflessness, they sometimes react as if I've asked them to put their house on the market or give away all their money. If there were a self that existed in the way we think, discovering selflessness *would* be like putting our house on the market. But in the Buddhist tradition, the discovery of selflessness is called "completely joyful." It's not called "the raw end of the deal," or "I'd rather go back to bed," or "This is scary and depressing."

I remember rising from my meditation seat one day and

being struck by the transparency of the world's appearances. This was not like being in some kind of dream or god realm. It felt like a balance between groundedness and fluidity. I could no longer solidify every thought, every word, every appearance, because the transitory quality of myself and everything around me—the lack of substance—was so vivid. My mind felt buoyant and joyful, because it was open, free from concept.

When we separate ourselves from the world and imagine that "me" has to conquer it, we are paupers who think that there is something to subjugate, own, or manipulate. Because we are objectifying the world, we see it as a threat and we defend ourselves against it. With the virtue of knowing selflessness, we are pulling the rug out from under the world's ability to terrorize and confuse us. Truly ruling our world is seeing the world for what it is—constantly shifting appearances that we attempt to freeze with assumptions and expectations. It is moving waves and particles that, like the illusion of "me," we take as real and solid. The selflessness of the dragon understands that the world is appearing, but that, at its heart, those appearances are empty. In reality, there is no world to rule. We are ruling a dream, and we are all sharing the same dream.

Discovering the selfless nature doesn't have a monumental "Eureka!" quality. It is more like being continually perplexed, the way we feel when we're looking for the car keys we're so sure are in our pocket, or when the supermarket's being renovated and what we need has moved to a different aisle each time we go shopping. That experience of being somewhat dumbfounded is the beginning of wisdom. We can no longer believe what our negative emotions are telling us, because prajna is bringing us in tune with deeper truths. We're beginning to see through our ignorance—the everyday vigil we sustain to confirm that we exist in some permanent way. We look at our mind and see that it is a fluid situation, and we look at the world and see that it is a fluid situation. Our expectation of permanence is confounded.

Glimpsing selflessness requires us to penetrate reality, as every enlightened ruler has done. If we are to rule our world—generate compassion without attachment—we too will have to embark on this monumental quest. The starting point is our contemplation. Seeing clearly how things are on the relative level takes us toward the truth about how things are at the ultimate level. It loosens our discursive mind and lets prajna emerge. We can sit and contemplate, "If I have a self, where is it? Is it inside me, or outside me?" As we contemplate, a little prajna pokes out its head. It's a feeling that maybe that sense of self is not really there. We have let go of our concept for just a moment. We are having a glimpse into reality. In Tibet, people write poetry about this experience.

We can only understand the truth of emptiness by contemplating a concept like the self. Placing our mind on this concept and contemplating it is like a taking a spaceship to the sun, which is wisdom. As we get closer to the sun, the heat of wisdom ignites the concept. Finally there is no concept, and we realize the empty, ungraspable nature of everything, beyond the four extremes of existence, nonexistence, neither, or both. This is how we arrive at an understanding of emptiness. There is no way that concept can land on wisdom, but we have to use concept to get there.

It helps to have a teacher to point us in the direction of the truth and give us a description of the way to see it accurately. For example, "If the accurate understanding of selflessness were a person, it would look like this." Contemplation is like taking that picture and finding the face that matches it. Once we find that person, our job is to live with her, get to know her intimately, and marry her. Our bond is finally cemented with the first child, which is our realization. It means we have internalized the truth of selflessness. Understanding one thing, we understand all things. We are no longer fooled. Seeing the world in the light of ultimate prajna, the Great Eastern Sun, we know that all is basic goodness. This is the royal view.

19

The Confidence of Wisdom

The mind of the dragon speaks a different language than does the mind caught in hope and fear.

SITTING IN A MOUNTAIN CAVE in Tibet, gazing down into endless valleys, I could see why that country is known as the "rooftop of the world." Far below me, animals and villagers tarried through the day, their view limited by the walls of the valley and their daily needs. Expanding my mind across the horizon from high on the mountain, I encountered no such obstructions. My mind felt big and free, a reflection of the sky in all its vastness. This vast place where sky meets earth is where the dragon plays.

When I came to the West and heard about knights slaying dragons, I was shocked. In Tibet, the dragon symbolizes incomprehensible profundity. "Profound" is the depth of our vast and fathomless mind. To know profundity is to know basic goodness. It is self-existing, without beginning or end. It is beyond conditions. It is victorious in every situation, because it is not manufactured. It cuts through all concepts. With profundity, we can look at people and see all the games they're playing, as if their manipulation is a suit they are wearing to cover their basic goodness. Understanding reality, we are less gullible.

The mind of the dragon speaks a different language than does the small mind caught in hope and fear. The claustrophobic mind is unable to read the signs of this profound wisdom; because it believes in "me," it speaks the language of aggression. If we're angry or jealous and somebody is full of compassion, we simply cannot comprehend his accommodation and love. He is residing in the brilliant mind of the dragon, and we're being tormented by the drip of the dark age. When we finally relax, we realize that our anger was for nothing. From a distance, we can even see the humor in it. Now our mind is gaining elevation. It is coming closer to the principle of dragon. We feel the vastness of mind and wonder how we could have gone to the valley's depth.

The wisdom of the dragon transcends duality. Seeing through the illusion of duality means we have made friends with the world. We no longer divide the world between "this" and "that," or "I want" and "I don't want." We see wisdom as who we are, and as who others are. When somebody walks into the room, we don't feel threatened; we feel curious. In using the strategies of the tiger, lion, and garuda, we've developed precision in how we relate to our mind, and we're more open to the world. Now, with the mind of the dragon, we are open to whatever the world presents, taking interest in its every detail. This open-mindedness and precision are the ingredients of fearlessness. Instead of defending ourselves against others, we feel inquisitive. How do they talk? How do they behave? How do they present themselves?

From working with our own mind, we know that we all have a little scheme called "me." Now we can see this clearly in others. She's too well assembled, too perfect. Or there's an air of forced relaxation. Perhaps she wants to help, but is trapped by hesitation. Something's not straightforward; there is something she's not saying. Does she want power, confirmation, or just to be left alone? We're using relative prajna to see what's going on. When we see the game that someone's playing, we're curious about that, too. We don't solidify it. Our wisdom comes from knowing we can learn from her, and therefore we can help her. Working with others, we are working with ourselves. That's emptiness and compassion. It's no longer "me" against "you." The boundary has dissolved.

This sky of a mind is the result of the tiger's contentment, the lion's joy, and the garuda's equanimity. We are living in a very big place. Anything is possible, because we're using exertion, discipline, and generosity to keep stepping through the hesitation called "me." We appreciate everybody and everything. With the selflessness of the dragon, we can harness anything we experience to propel us along the path of confidence, as if it were wind in our sails. We radiate confidence naturally, like the sun shining. We are not clinging to a concept of what we hope or fear will next arise.

The Buddha says, "Now contemplate that all of us are Buddha—totally enlightened beings. The word *buddha* means 'awake.' " A buddha wakes up and sees that everything is awake. It's like waking up from a deep sleep—the world looks different. That is clear seeing in its most sublime capacity. We conclude that yes, we are awake, an enlightened king or queen. This certainty in the bigness of our being is the wisdom mind of the dragon, the luminous intelligence of the Great Eastern Sun.

With the wisdom mind of the dragon, life itself becomes the source of our energy. The more we are involved with our life, the more energy we have. We actually become younger, because we are less burdened, less jaded. When we start a new project or meet a new friend, we don't think, "Here we go again. I've already done this a million times." We have an open mind that is genuinely and continually engaged, without any kind of pre-thought.

The dragon dances with the elements of every situation. When people are irritating, we're amused, because we understand that what's irritating us is our own irritation, which is fluid and empty. Others can't comprehend how somebody could be so simple and cheerful. They are sitting at the same table, perceiving what we are perceiving, but caught in self-protective mind, they perceive the world as hard and unfriendly. Their minds feel tight, the opposite of spacious, because they are in pain.

Others might even find the inscrutability of the ruler to be freakish, out of touch with reality. The mind of "me" can't understand the profound reality of the dragon. But the dragon understands the suffering of the mind of "me." For people whose minds are plagued by doubt, reality is unstable since it will change from today to tomorrow. From the perspective of the dragon, they look like children, happy and sad over meaningless things; like insane people, chasing mirages, wishing to express their love but suffering needlessly. Therefore we must be merciful and try to awaken their vastness.

The dragon mind feels a unity with the environment that allows us to perceive the world in an elemental way. Like the elements, the confidence of the dragon doesn't have to be created or propped up. This wisdom sees water for water, earth for earth, fire for fire, and wind for wind. We are not surprised by change, and when it occurs, we can be like water and flow. When it is time to be solid like the earth, we can be steadfast. When the heat of enthusiasm is necessary, we are like the fire of all fires. We can blow with the wind of virtue, uplifting any situation. Or we can rest in space, accommodating everything. This is the power of a king or queen—the warrior of all warriors.

When we plug into our elemental richness, there is a sense of total empowerment. We are electrified with ziji, the glory of our being. We can do whatever we want—not because we have figured out how to dominate everybody but because we are fearless. Our windhorse is completely liberated. With this kind of confidence, we hold the future in our hands.

The dragon is sometimes shown holding the jewel of auspiciousness. This is the enlightened heart and mind of the king and queen. With the wisdom of the dragon, we discover that the Rigden and ourselves are the same. Our wisdom, compassion, and courage are no longer a myth. Once we possess this jewel, our life becomes blessed. Because of our openness and precision, causes and conditions come together naturally, like the elements, to create success and accomplishment.

20

Attracting Auspiciousness

A mind that knows its own depth can see the brilliant, elemental magic of the world.

WITH THE SELFLESSNESS and wisdom of the dragon, we are in a stable, open space, no longer derailed by the delusion of duality. We become sensitive to the subtle energies of the environment, and they become sensitive to us, because our senses are open to all the realms. As we take in the suffering of others, we join the intuitive wisdom of prajna with the practicality of compassion. Our windhorse is strong; we are drinking ziji for breakfast. Now we are able to judge conditions and time decisions properly in order to give new endeavors the greatest possible advantage for success. Because we are in tune with it, the environment becomes reflective in our decision making, shutting the door in our face or providing what we need to go forward. As the golfer Ben Hogan once said, "The more I practice, the luckier I get." In Tibet, this luck is known as *tashi tendrel*—auspicious coincidence.

When I visited Tibet, people were constantly offering me gifts, a customary way to make a karmic connection with a lama. Since I am considered to be the rebirth of Mipham Rinpoche, one of the most revered teachers in Tibet, many people wanted to make such a connection. I was offered horses, herds of yak, fabric, grains, and land. I kept telling people that I appreciated their gesture, but that on this trip, I was just visiting and observing. It was not the time for me to accept big gifts.

At the end of the journey, we arrived at the valley of Magyal Pomra, where the legendary warrior-king Gesar, one of my ancestors, lived and ruled. In addition, when the previous Mipham Rinpoche had visited this area, he told the people that he would return. Taking my arrival as the fulfillment of his promise, the local residents offered me a mountain and a valley in which to build a monastery. They were so fervent in their request that I said I would climb to the mountaintop, and if I saw any auspicious signs, I would consider accepting their gift. So off I went. When I reached the top of the mountain, three rainbows appeared, which put me in an awkward position. All of the people and monks were smiling broadly, and I had no choice but to accept.

The Buddha taught that all things are interdependent; nothing comes about on its own accord. The more we conduct ourselves with wisdom and compassion, the more auspicious our lives become. It is as if drala were offering us a gift. By acting virtuously, exerting ourselves in service to others, we are blessed in return by harmony and good luck.

Auspicious coincidences lead us toward joy and freedom by presenting us with circumstances that will further our realization and understanding. They can lead us to a spiritual teacher, a lover, or a new friend who will change our life. For example, the poet Allen Ginsberg met my father, who became his teacher, while they were trying to hail the same taxicab on a street in Manhattan.

As we continue our training in rulership, tashi tendrel—auspicious coincidence—increases. A mind that knows its own depth can see the brilliant, elemental magic of the world. The world communicates to us because we're available, like a flower in spring. Conditions are ripe, and the flower opens. Wisdom and compassion attune us to life, and the environment responds.

Each situation that comes together with auspiciousness shows us how we can step forward—not backward or sideways—into the limitless light of the Great Eastern Sun. Causes and conditions meet in such a way that we know when it's time to take action—or not. When we're awake enough to see what the world is presenting, conditions can show us the right time to build a house, start school, or expand our business.

In Tibet, when people are about to do a meditation retreat, they consider all the signs that might indicate when the retreat should begin and where it should be. If we are looking at a particular place and someone offers us flowers or we

run into a friend, that is tendrel. Or perhaps somebody un-
expectedly says something encouraging and positive. These
signs might indicate that the time is right to do a retreat in
that area. Similarly, if we are looking at a place and a light-
bulb burns out, or we see a dead bird or hear people arguing,
we might conclude that the place is inappropriate. An ad-
vanced practitioner whose meditation is deeply rooted will
be less affected by the environment, and might even specifi-
cally choose to meditate in a difficult location in order to
become stronger. But for most of us, having an inviting situation is incredibly important, because we already have plenty
of difficulties and obstacles to overcome.

When we approach our difficulties aggressively—thinking that if we just push hard enough, something is bound to
give way—we become proud and stubborn. Drip obscures
our vision, and it is difficult to perceive the signals that the
world is sending us. We're so wrapped up in speed or worry
that we've still got our umbrella up, even though it's not rain-
ing anymore. At times like that, we aren't present to hear
what the world is telling us.

Once after spending several months with my teacher
Khyentse Rinpoche, I was returning to the West. On the day
I left for the airport at Kathmandu, everything was difficult.
First I had trouble getting there, and then, when I was at the
airport, there were hassles with my passport and my luggage.
Because I was committed to teaching a series of meditation
workshops, I pressed onward. In my hurry to return to my
responsibilities, I was not looking clearly at what the environment was telling me.

It was such a relief when I was finally on the plane. In Nepal and India, however, you're never really there until you're there. As we taxied down the runway, we heard a loud bang—one of those sounds you never want to hear on an airplane. The pilot brought the plane to a screeching stop ten feet from the end of the runway—in Kathmandu, a drop off a high precipice. One of the engines had blown up. Everyone was completely silent as we taxied back to the terminal. We were lucky that no one had been hurt.

Right away I sent a message to Rinpoche, telling him what had happened. He replied that I should return to the monastery immediately. There were obstacles, especially because this was the end of the lunar year, considered a time of change. My teaching on wisdom and compassion would also attract obstacles, just as it had for the Buddha.

Rinpoche wanted me to delay my trip for three days. During that time, we performed meditations and rituals, and he bestowed empowerments on me to help strengthen my windhorse, clear my vision, and overcome obstacles. We did the *lhasang*—the juniper-smoke ceremony—several times. As we concluded, I felt rejuvenated. Now it felt like the proper time to leave. With a relaxed mind and invigorated windhorse, I entered the new year with enthusiasm.

Auspicious occurrences indicate that our mind is beginning to relax into the present moment. When we are able to relax, we realize that the present moment is all there is. What we think of as the past is only a present memory, and what we think of as the future is a projection of the present. The wisdom of the dragon tells us to slow down, let go, and be present for the moment, for that is where all power and magic lie.

I am always struck by the awesome power generated by my teachers. Such genuine presence—wangthang—attracts auspiciousness. This is not ordinary charisma that comes and goes with conventional success and failure. At times, it is gentle and deep; at other times, it is like heat radiating from a dormant volcano. They are different from other important people. Their presence is big and stable. Sometimes looking at them is like staring into the sun; their brilliance is overwhelming. The source of their power is a deep understanding of their minds. Since they are devoted to the benefit of all sentient beings, I am certain that to some degree such people magnetize tashi tendrel for everyone.

When Gerald Red Elk, a Sioux medicine man, came to meet my father, we were in the middle of a meditation program at Shambhala Mountain Center, where we were all living in tents. This was the meeting of two great wisdom lineages. It was very dramatic. First there was an incredible thunderstorm that cleared the air. It was so intense that everybody knew something important was happening. The minute Gerald Red Elk arrived, the storm stopped. Every cloud disappeared. When these two warriors touched heads in greeting under a completely blue sky, it was like a new day. We knew that the connection had been made, and that it was good. Each of these rulers was standing on a powerhouse of virtue, and their meeting illuminated the environment with lightning and sunshine.

VI

THE CONFIDENCE

OF RULERSHIP

21

Ruling from the
Ground Up

Within my body I have this incredible
confidence—contentment, joy, equanimity,
and wisdom.

T HIS SIMPLE CONTEMPLATION on the four kinds
of confidence was born one morning when I was doing
my daily exercises. It occurred to me that the tiger, lion,
garuda, and dragon are not just concepts that inspire us toward rulership. Their energies are reflected within our own
bodies, where joining heaven and earth begins. This exercise
is called "ground lungta," because we do it lying down, relax-
ing, with our eyes closed. We can use it to raise windhorse
before entering our daily life.

We start with the feet, imagining that they are the tiger,

which is orange, representing the confidence of contentment. Contentment comes from being discerning and appreciative. The tiger moves with large cushioned feet through the jungle, across the earth, and through the grass. It isn't walking carefully because it is afraid. It is present for every step because it respects its environment. As rulers we have total respect for how virtue moves us forward and nonvirtue moves us backward. We know that ruling from the mind of "What about me?" does not bring happiness.

We sometimes know what we should not do, and we do it anyway. Sometimes we know what we should do, and we cannot do it. Exertion is the key to engaging with virtue and moving forward. By imagining our feet and legs as the tiger, we are connecting with the earth of our day, remembering our precious human life, and deciding to use it well.

Next we move our awareness up to the area inside our body just below the navel. In this place, we have heat. This is the lion, which is white and represents discipline, delight, and energy. The lion has tremendous joy, because it is no longer burdened by bewilderment. It knows that virtue brings the warmth of the Great Eastern Sun and that nonvirtue brings the heaviness of the setting sun. Virtue elevates us above confusion and heaviness; the mind is liberated from doubt. We are able to frolic in the joy of the highlands, because we have certainty that helping others leads to happiness. When we offer the fire of this discipline and joy, the world reflects it back to us. Extending compassion to others strengthens windhorse.

Now we place our awareness on our chest and arms. This area is the garuda, which is red, the confidence of equanimity, a mind that has no boundaries. The garuda is outrageous because it has gone beyond the conventional way of doing things, which is to be totally fixated, totally attached. The most outrageous thing we can do in this world is to accept what happens and fly with it.

We are often living with a sense of fear. When we enter our day, we don't know if we're going to fall or fly. The garuda knows that fear is a projection of fixed mind. There is no boundary to space. When we are free of fixed mind, like a newly hatched garuda, we can expand our wings—our arms—and embrace the present moment. This is how we attract the blessing of drala.

In this dark age, we all need as much drala energy as we can get. Sometimes simply cleaning our room, our desk, or our car is a way to attract drala. Removing the clutter from our environment and making it sparkle cheers us up. Just from a little situation like that, we can invite drala. From a conventional point of view, that seems very outrageous. But the ruler knows that enriching the world with care and appreciation is how we live a life in which we are always moving forward.

Finally we move our awareness to the head and shoulders; they represent the selfless confidence of the dragon, which is blue. The confidence of the dragon is wisdom that transcends concept. With prajna, we are no longer fooled by appearances. We have abandoned small mind—using negative emotions to get what we want, trying to manipulate the world into our corner—for the mind of the Great Eastern Sun. "Great" means that we know the vast profundity of our mind and heart. "Eastern" means that our wisdom is perpetually available—always arising and waking us up. "Sun" means brilliance, lack of ignorance. Great Eastern Sun is what we all possess, but at a dualistic and conceptual level, the mind of the Great Eastern Sun cannot be comprehended, so to others our wisdom is inscrutable.

At this point, we place our awareness back on our feet and say to ourselves softly and slowly, KI KI. Then we move our awareness up to the area below our navel and say SO SO. Then to the chest and arms—KI KI. And finally to the head and shoulders—SO SO. These are very old syllables used by Shambhala warriors to invoke drala. As we say them, windhorse begins to percolate and rise. We visualize the orange tiger, the white lion, the red garuda, and the blue dragon dissolving into our heart center, into the Great Eastern Sun. We open our eyes, sit up, and imagine the warmth of the Great Eastern Sun expanding everywhere.

We finish with the warrior cry: ASHE, LHA GYAL LO. *Ashe* is the embodiment of fearlessness—the primordial confidence that cuts through doubt. *Lha* implies something high up, divine. *Gyal* means "victorious." When we say, "May heaven be victorious," we are increasing our ability to rise above negativity. We are saying, "Within my body I have this incredible confidence—contentment, joy, equanimity, and wisdom. That is totally victorious and wonderful."

We also could say, "Oh, but it's just the feet and blood and bones and the guts and the head and the brain." It's true, it is completely physical. But from the inner perspective, in terms of windhorse, we are contemplating specific parts of the body to invoke drala. That's how Milarepa, the Tibetan yogic saint, could fly. We probably won't be doing that any time soon—unless we're getting on an airplane—but in using the same principle, we are bringing windhorse—the energy of awakened mind—into every molecule of our being. This is how we invite drala into our day.

Having completed our practice, we can get up and engage with our life. We can meditate, make a latte, take a shower, kiss our spouse or partner, say good morning to our children, or turn on the news. We can do this practice at any time of day, of course, even when we are standing, sitting, or walking. With the confidence of the Great Eastern Sun, no matter what time it is, we will rise and shine.

22

Ruling with Wisdom

By resting in a big mind, we can conquer small mind.

W HEN I FORMALLY assumed my responsibilities as a sakyong, I was to lead one of the largest meditation communities in the West, as well as take my seat as a spiritual leader in Tibet. I saw two elements: possibility and chaos. Although I had always known I would eventually take this role, it was only now that I could fully see the issues at hand. There was factionalism. Also, I was young. Many people I was to lead had been students of my father; they had strong opinions about how I should proceed. Newer students wanted to change how things were done. There were also financial issues. In addition, people were coming to me with their personal problems and business concerns. I was to guide people on their meditative journeys as well. I was also acting as a cultural bridge. The Tibetans wanted me to behave in a traditional way. They were concerned that I was spending too much time with Westerners. The Westerners thought that I was paying too much attention to Tibetans and the old ways. It would have been easy to feel crushed by the weight of these responsibilities. How was I to create harmony?

The Buddha taught Dawa Sangpo, the first king of Shambhala, how to rule by joining heaven and earth. Earth is where we live, and heaven gives us the ability to live with meaning. Following the paths of the tiger, lion, garuda, and dragon, we learn to balance heaven (wisdom and equanimity) with earth (contentment and delight in helping others). Then we are all-victorious, able to accomplish what we want, by ruling our world every day. The Shambhala teachings tell us that to join heaven and earth, we need to be benevolent, true, genuine, fearless, artful, and rejoicing. These are the six ways of ruling.

The first three ways of ruling—being benevolent, true, and genuine—are related to heaven. They are qualities of justness. Being just arises from wisdom, unwavering certainty in basic goodness. This is the first step in bringing heaven down to earth. We have discovered our own sanity by conquering confusion. People look up to us because our life has purpose. Our presence is benevolent, true, and genuine, like a beam of light breaking through the clouds.

Benevolence is rooted in patience, which results in gentleness, absence of aggression. Our mind is spacious because we have total confidence in it. This is not blind compassion or an anything-goes attitude. As rulers, we understand that people suffer, which connects us with the earth. We use the tiger's exertion to keep our feet on the ground. Earth gives us purpose. It's saying, "Since the sakyong is the earth-protector, bringing peace, compassion, and wisdom to earth is your responsibility."

If we want to fulfill our mandate, we can't take suffering too personally. If we take it too personally, we lose touch with heaven. We become attached, letting every scenario draw us in. Our mind becomes a little box. We begin to panic because we have no room to maneuver. For example, a project is taking longer than expected and our colleague starts blaming us. We become angry. Our benevolence begins to dissolve. We make excuses, or perhaps we blame someone else. We're up against the wall, and aggression is putting us there. Our windhorse weakens, and our doubt strengthens. Basic goodness seems like a myth; wisdom, compassion, and courage seem like faint ideals. At this point we don't need to be less gentle—we need to be more gentle. That panic is telling us that we're holding on too tightly. It's time to let go into space, like the garuda. Then we can play like the dragon, moving with the elements as they arise.

In my situation, I felt like first I needed to listen to all the problems and perspectives. I could just let people express themselves. I tried to be open-minded and inquisitive. Some people were friendly, and some were aggressive. In both cases, I got a closer look into people's minds. I learned that when others are acting out of aggression and speed, they can't quite trust benevolence. Small mind cannot understand big mind, so the wisdom ruler often encounters blame and criticism. Others try to usurp our power by moving us away from being gentle, attempting to hook us into negative emotion. But gentleness is always the best whip, one that everyone respects, because it is devoted to the welfare of others.

Benevolence requires the steadiness of an elephant—a sense of trusting ourselves and remembering the suffering of others—because it is easy to become irritated with people. If we feel cornered in the hallway by irritation, it seems overwhelming, and we're likely to react aggressively. Since we're trapped not in a building but only within the confines of our mind, we can be patient. Patience creates space beyond the logical conclusion of negative emotion, like a large meadow in which our irritation can stomp around. After a while, it looks silly.

In some situations, being wrathful might appear to be the most compassionate thing we can do. At such times, we need to look carefully at our mind and heart and ask, "Is this really compassion? Or is it negativity in disguise?" Discernment stands back and takes a look at what is happening before acting. Discipline remembers the delight of helping others. Equanimity releases attachment and concept. Wisdom knows that we will often make mistakes; our training in rulership is ongoing and never-ending. If we want to know whether our wrath is compassionate, we can look at the result: the result of compassion is joy and happiness; the result of anger is that our reputation suffers, and those around us are hurt and stressed.

Benevolence is infused with being true, the second way of ruling. We are true to ourselves in moving forward on the path of virtue. We will not be deterred. This is conviction grounded in confidence, like the force behind a strong breeze. The breeze might be warm and pleasant, but it is constantly moving. Being true to the strategies of tiger, lion, garuda, and dragon grounds our benevolence. Without the unshakable quality of being true, benevolence becomes protocol or politics.

Being benevolent and true to the view of basic goodness gives us natural diplomacy. Having worked diligently with our own mind, we're familiar with realms of anger, jealousy, and ignorance, as well as those of generosity and joy. We can see where people are coming from and what their tactics are, and we know what game they are playing.

Even our friends will sometimes try to manipulate us or reinterpret our intentions in order to mask their incompetence or insecurity. If we are true, they will soon discover that this behavior doesn't work, because our gentleness is weighted with conviction. We no longer believe that we can get what we want with negativity. We're using different strategies. We understand how power flows: by resting in a big mind, we can conquer small mind.

With benevolence as our base, the spirit of being true will strengthen and build. It is a process of constantly sharpening our wisdom on the whetstone of experience. It can be lonely. Our connection with heaven gives us the strength to make decisions without feeling doubt, but at times we have to make decisions that others don't like. In my own situation, people are quite liberal in giving me advice. One person's advice is always contradicting another's. It would be easy to crumble under the weight of others' hopes and fears. In the end, whatever the issue is, I have to be just. "Just" means not straying from the path of virtue.

Being benevolent and true is how to arrive at genuineness—the third way of ruling. This is not even *our* genuineness particularly. It is just genuine, a star in the sky that everyone can see. We all recognize the truth when we see it. With a mind elevated by wisdom and anchored in a noble heart, we know we're doing the right thing, because whether we're a ruler or a pauper, it is the right thing to do. If we're in doubt, we need to reconnect with being benevolent and true. With these three ways of ruling, whatever we do will be just.

When we are just, others are willing to carry out our wishes. The Sanskrit word for spiritual teacher—*guru*— connotes heaviness, a deep understanding. When my teachers speak, even ordinary words seem laden with meaning and potency. This kind of power carries a natural command—a penetrating influence that is neither a threat nor a trick. Clearly, truth is being expressed, so we listen.

23

Ruling with Power

Our power comes not from suppressing others but from uplifting them.

RECENTLY I ASKED STANLEY, a scriptwriter friend of mine, about the movie business. He said, "It's so transparent, so elusive. Even if you did something great before, if you're not doing something now, people treat you as a has-been. It's exhausting to keep up your power, which is very short-lived." The king and queen know that power that depends on manipulation of circumstances is not genuine power. Power that depends on bombarding others with our ambition or terrorizing them into submission does not last, because it requires constant maintenance.

In order to be genuinely powerful, the ruler balances the next three ways of ruling: fearlessness, artfulness, and rejoicing. These three connect us to earth. True power is grounded in fearlessness, a natural expression of our confidence, knowledge, and understanding. We are fearless in jumping into our own wisdom, because we are beyond doubt about basic goodness. We are not afraid of the power of windhorse, which brings worldly and spiritual success. Because it does not need to prove itself, this fearlessness has a gentle quality, rooted in unwavering compassion.

If we fear our own power, we have lost our connection with heaven. As a result, we lose our connection to earth, and we become political. Then, like fools, we think that we need to manipulate or steal the power of others, imagining that someone else has something we need, and that going after it is how to obtain it. Because conventional politics is rooted in fear, power rooted in politics doesn't last. Others see that we're not being totally honest, and our lack of stability becomes a weak piece they can wiggle.

If we fear the power of others, we have lost our connection with earth. Trying to rule our world single-handedly, we are not really ruling. We are giving up. We may believe that independence is a sign of power, but not wanting to work with others is a sign that we haven't conquered self-absorption. We're saying, "I don't want to work with others, because it makes me angry. It takes too much patience. People are stupid." The reality is that we can't handle our anger, we can't develop our patience, and we can't cultivate our wisdom without working with others. How can we practice not yelling when we're angry if there's no one around to push our buttons?

We have to be fearless in making decisions. The decision may concern something that affects a whole community, like determining a course of study, or it may concern something that affects only one person, like deciding what time we're going to be home so that our partner can use the car. Making decisions in a tentative way—especially since the anxiety of others often manifests as criticism—only creates more fear. Our own fear can create havoc in our business, family, relationship, or country. If our fear translates into reticence, people will pay no attention to our words. If our fear translates into being heavy-handed and forceful, they will resent our power and resist us. We have to be fearless, because people are depending on our power. That power comes not from suppressing others but from uplifting them. Fear is a state of mind. Fearlessness is our nature. In ruling from fearlessness, we are ruling from our roots. Like fear, fearlessness can spread.

Some years ago, when we were planning to expand our facilities at Shambhala Mountain Center, people in the administration were hesitant. They came up with all sorts of reasons that building was not a good idea. They asked me, "Are you sure that this is all going to work?" Underneath their hesitation was fear. I told them that, as elders in positions of power, they had to be fearless, because our intention is to benefit others.

The next aspect of power is artfulness. Rulership is an art. The enlightened king and queen know how to balance power's inner and outer aspects, and they arrange the kingdom of their life accordingly. The circle of people around us gives us a base from which to generate power. As rulers we need domestic partners and family to promote decency in our home. We need ministers—administrative helpers and friends who promote our efforts to create harmony in the world. We need generals—fearless protectors in the guise of caring friends and teachers who remind us to hold the view of basic goodness.

Our circle of friends, family, and work associates is our treasury, because they provide a container in which we practice virtue. If we are to rule, we need someone to protect and care for. Working with others artfully engages all the strategies we've learned on the tiger, lion, garuda, dragon path. It hones our discernment, increases our exertion and discipline, enlarges our joy, engages our fearlessness, and sharpens our wisdom and skill.

Establishing the people around us in their positions is like wearing jewelry. Certain pieces go on the head and others on the wrists. The king and queen use discernment to reflect on the qualities of each person and determine her or his place. We might appreciate the creativity of our friend who stays up until all hours writing television shows, but that kind of creativity isn't what we'd look for in choosing an accountant. Some friends we reflect deeply with, confiding our innermost concerns; with others we only play golf. There are people at work whom we greatly appreciate, but we would never invite them to our home.

Some people in our circle will be able to take on more responsibility; others would be overwhelmed by it. Which of our siblings can be responsible for the care of our aging parents? There will be different times for different people. Our assistant was a perfect trainee when he was fresh out of school, but now he is bored. Shall we move him into a more challenging position? Fitting the person with the position with the time—this results in harmony. Good people in good positions increase good fortune like a wish-fulfilling tree.

Choosing the wrong person for a position will hurt the kingdom as a whole. Putting a small-minded person in a position of influence is like having a leak that requires continuous attention. That person's lack of synergy with others will drain the windhorse of the entire situation. If our mother or child marries someone who influences her in a negative way, for example, the windhorse of our family will weaken.

Putting someone with bad behavior in a high position only fuels further bad behavior. If we choose to work for an employer who encourages us to lie or steal, our windhorse will erode. So will everyone else's; one person's negativity has the power to sabotage the collective inspiration, and obstacles will arise. With people properly chosen and the harmony that naturally grows, everyone becomes powerful, and our work proceeds smoothly.

Artfulness has the tiger's payu, discernment. We continually examine the influences in our environment. If we favor people with money, we will contort our principles. Then virtue is no longer ruling; money is ruling. Similarly, if we favor close friends and consorts, desire will begin to rule.

When we are manipulated by our own attachment, our windhorse spirals downward. If everyone in our circle flatters or agrees with us, our self-awareness will become cloudy, like a faded mirror. We will lose our ability to determine what to cultivate and what to discard. If we listen to rumors and slander, we will begin to take sides. This will create friction, which makes an aggressive environment.

Acting artfully means we know what we are going to say and what it means to others. Before we speak, we ask ourselves, "How will this help?" We determine whether we should talk to our mother or our father first. Always considering others, we communicate our wishes with impeccable skill and timing. We may have good news for our family, our business. We're going to change neighborhoods; there's a new product on the horizon. If we bombard people with our inspiration, it loses its effectiveness. We need to allow space in which they can absorb the information. If we are overly anxious in the beginning, or too exuberant, others may back off. If we hesitate in relating the news to others, they may feel hurt that we didn't tell them sooner. A conversation here, a conversation there—as small as it may seem—builds harmony all around. When we know a change is on the way, well-timed words to our parents, our children, our neighbors, our secretary, our boss—all reflect consideration. What distinguishes this kind of communication from manipulation is that it is not clandestine. Many people are afraid of change. If we are artful with our power, they will see our fearlessness and grow from it.

Consideration of others is the root of being artful. This

is consideration based on trying to be genuine, not on fear of stepping on people's toes. In that case, we are ruling not from fearlessness but from fear of retribution. If we fear retribution, we are hiding something. We fear being exposed. Then we are not conducting ourselves from the genuine source of power—emptiness and compassion beyond attachment to "me."

In the practice of artfulness, we're considering how best to help others, not how best to avoid hurting their feelings. Of course, we must be sensitive to how others are feeling. Peter the Great once dressed as a commoner in order to listen to the needs of the people with open ears. Similarly, the more confidence we have in our own wisdom and compassion, the more artful we will be in listening to others and knowing how to help them. We should ask questions, because answers often reveal both good and bad intention.

With artfulness, we open a difficult situation up with wisdom rather than close it down with our own negativity. We want to draw people out, not suppress them. When people have acted badly, we can ask, "What do you think happened?" "Did this behavior bring the result you wanted?" "How did it make you feel?" "Would you like to do things differently?" Instead of forcing our opinion on them, we try to create space in which they can learn to use discernment and discipline to discover their own wisdom. The questions we ask are often as important as the answers we offer.

We are artful in acknowledging the virtuous efforts of others, even if their work is not obvious to anyone else.

When people do good work, we offer appreciation, praise, affection, or a gift. Our encouragement brings delight; it infuses their work with meaning. When people are feeling discouraged, we foster inspiration. On a journey in Tibet, it is traditional to stop and look back to see how far we have come. Pausing and reviewing our accomplishment strengthens our resolve to keep going. Sometimes we can encourage people by helping them see their priorities more clearly, with the motivation of leading them to a more positive state of mind.

In order to get things done, sometimes we have to go slowly, and sometimes we have to move quickly. But with artfulness, whatever the pace of our activity, it looks seamless. This kind of power stems from our genuine appreciation of the moment—from how we drink a cup of tea to how we wear our clothing. In ancient Japan, samurai warriors mastered many arts—flower arranging, tea ceremony, and conversation. They were able to contain their power in the most delicate of activities. A cup of tea conveyed the warmth of perfect friendship, an arrangement of flowers brought the cosmos into a dish. With the same elegance, they could draw their sword and strike a fatal blow, or release an arrow and pierce the heart of an enemy. Such perfect balance and timing attracts drala. It overtakes others before they know it, like the sun moving from morning to midday. When people feel our warmth, they are delighted. This is the art of power.

After we have studied Buddhist metaphysics and practiced debate for long hours, my teacher Penor Rinpoche often calls me out to share some tea. We talk about birds, the weather, or flowers. He loves to talk about animals. He is balancing my intellectual training with the art of conversation, which involves the equanimity of the garuda, letting go of our own concerns and making space to hear what others have to say. Whether physical or intellectual, power has to be balanced. Expressing it artfully creates harmony.

When we communicate power artfully, everyone feels included, as if we have each person's interests in mind. Because our power is not oppressive, communication is healthy and open. We feel fortunate in one another. This love brings the delight of the snow lion, because virtue gives birth to virtue. From the ground up, virtue manifests as basic decency—respect for the environment and care for each other. We have fearlessly rejected self-absorption, so joy and celebration arise. This brings us to the sixth way of ruling—rejoicing.

At Shambhala meditation retreats, both teachers and participants are working the principles of the tiger, lion, garuda, and dragon. We try to maintain our connection to heaven—confidence in basic goodness. We try to ground our view in earth—our everyday activity. In bringing heaven and earth together, we're attempting to generate harmony and create an enlightened world.

At the end of these programs, there is always a celebration. Inevitably, a series of toasts arises. Students toast teachers and meditation instructors in appreciation of their guidance; meditation instructors and teachers toast students in appreciation of the challenges and dedication they offered.

This isn't the only time I feel the sense of rejoicing and celebration in our community, but in this dark age, when it's so easy to succumb to aggression, our mutual exchange feels very powerful. It reflects how hard we are working together.

When I walk into a room where one of my teachers is sitting, I often feel as if I have just missed some kind of celebration. There is an air of crescendo. It's not that anything special is happening; I have just walked in on a cheerful, uncluttered state of mind—the tiger's contentment, the lion's delight, the garuda's equanimity, and the dragon's selflessness, all in one. My father exuded an air of celebration that included a big smile and a sense of playfulness and invitation. A ball of tsampa—roasted barley flour—from my teacher Khyentse Rinpoche tasted more delicious to me than a piece of chocolate cake.

The natural celebratory energy of balancing heaven and earth can arise anywhere. Celebration can be spontaneous or formal. We can put on some music and dance, or we can schedule a picnic in the country with our co-workers after we've finished a project together. When we have an important announcement to make, we can gather our friends and family for a special meal. We can express our joy by doing something we were scared to do before, or just by taking an afternoon off to see a movie with a friend. If celebration is missing in our life, we can take it as a sign that we have not been ruling our world. Our love and care are blocked. Negativity has crept in. We don't see anything to celebrate. When this happens, we need to remember basic goodness.

In Tibet, the lunar New Year—usually observed in February—is like Christmas, New Year's, Easter, and our birthdays all rolled into one. I asked an old Tibetan lama how he felt about the celebration as a child. He said, "Of course we were excited. We could barely sleep the night before. Not only was there the lhasang—the juniper-smoke ceremony—the many offerings, the ceremonies, but we also had a delicious meal." I wondered what that was, and he told me it was yak head. They would sit at the table and eat the aged and preserved innards of the yak—a far cry from ice cream and cake but a celebration, nonetheless.

Celebration is an attitude. We are happy in our skin. We are happy in our family. We are happy in our work. We are happy in our country. This is the ultimate appreciation of daily life. We're not just in it for ourselves; we're in it because we want to offer wisdom and compassion to others, who feel the power of our love and care. This kind of relationship with our kingdom creates harmony, a friction-free environment. As we overcome fear and aggression, there is less bickering, jealousy, and competition. Thus as a group we have strong windhorse, which makes us all-victorious.

24

Ruling Your World

When we create the right conditions for success,
windhorse doesn't just gallop, it flies.

T HE TRADITION OF RULERSHIP tells us that we are
all meant to rule our world. We don't have to rule the
entire world, but if we rule our own mind and thus our environment, our peace and power does in fact begin to spread
into the rest of the world. This energy is lungta, windhorse—spiritual and worldly success.

The teachings of Shambhala emphasize the reality that
we all have basic goodness, and that the world we live in has
basic goodness. However, in this dark age there is a constant
sense of fear and dissatisfaction. That negativity consumes
us so that we cannot settle even in our own mind, let alone
in our family or our society. When we are all saving the last
piece of pie for ourselves, we are constantly undermining the

possibility of creating stability and happiness. When we approach our planet with this attitude, the world is ruled by small-mindedness. Businesses and governments are crippled and ultimately fail, because everyone is on the "me" plan. Being dragged around by emotions destabilizes our mind, our day, our life, and ultimately, the welfare of our planet. That is the notion of suffering.

The ruler looks at that suffering with the intention of doing something about it. In Shambhala, we vow to create an "enlightened world." This vow reflects our aspiration to relieve suffering by awakening the world to its own potential.

After King Dawa Sangpo received the transmission of these teachings from the Buddha, he realized, as did all the Rigden kings, that in order for a society to be truly harmonious, it cannot be based on jealousy, greed, and anger. It must be rooted in a more primordial principle, something that cannot be bought and sold. Dawa Sangpo began to propagate the transmission he had received from the Buddha about basic goodness, the awakened nature of all. He taught his subjects to meditate and contemplate, and instructed them in the four strategies for bringing meaning to their lives. People became more peaceful, kind, and happy. Their confidence increased. Soon they were sleeping, eating, walking, and working according to the understanding of their indestructible nature. This is how the citizens of Shambhala discovered their own enlightenment.

Just as in the context of Buddhism we are all already buddha—"awake"—the world is already Shambhala. It is only because we are roaming in the kingdom of doubt and anger, jealousy and pride, that we cannot see it right now. When we see through our perpetual agitation and relax into basic goodness, the enlightened world of Shambhala begins to appear. Enlightenment is things as they are before we color them with our projections. When we take the vow of the ruler—to help create an enlightened world—we're saying that we're going to work in this life, right now, to develop confidence in basic goodness, so that we will be able to live in that sacred world, wherever we are.

There are no castes in the kingdom of Shambhala. We are all Rigden—"possessor of the family"—because we already possess our own awareness fully. To see this on the individual level, we need to wake up to the natural energy of our mind. Practicing meditation and contemplation is how we purify our mind, just as we polish a crystal ball so that we can actually see the full display of radiance. Understanding all as basic goodness, we take this life as our opportunity to be confident and free.

As a worldly path, Shambhala is grounded in doing what is best for society. The best thing for society, even in an everyday situation, is the complete fulfillment and happiness of the individual. If we want a world that generates love and happiness, we need to start watering the seeds of peace and stability in our own mind. By ruling our mind and using it to generate compassion, we can rule our economy and our future. The enlightened king and queen regard wealth as a measure of success, but to this they add the cause of true happiness. They know that happiness is never going to come just from physical forms, because happiness is a state of mind. With the wish-fulfilling jewel of wisdom and compassion as the basis of our life, we can develop this consciousness of happiness.

The enlightened kings and queens of the past, as well as the ascetics meditating in caves, have all said that the secret to creating stability is to put the welfare of others before our own. Some may consider this approach unrealistic. But the ruler knows that getting off the "me" plan is the most expedient and practical element in any economic system. An economy based on compassion infused with wisdom will not self-destruct. Trying to create stability without the foundation of these qualities will only condemn us to perpetual friction, and we will continue to pollute our world with the fumes of self-interest. The wish-fulfilling jewel is the best pollution control, because it brings spaciousness to the mind, which allows windhorse to arise.

Riding windhorse is how we use our worldly life as a spiritual path. We nurture heaven by developing certainty in basic goodness. We bring heaven down to earth by having the courage to act with compassion. Then we can live in the world as a ruler no matter what we are doing. We can be married, have children, and own a house. How we use our mind and live our life determine whether windhorse increases or diminishes. To rule our world is to live in a way that continually strengthens windhorse.

Windhorse brings spiritual and worldly success—personal power, harmony with others, strong life force, and material prosperity. It is connected with understanding how interdependence works. Like a good cook, we know that one ingredient does not create a delicious meal but that many elements must come together in exactly the right way. The ingredients for windhorse are mindfulness, awareness, and virtue, as well as the wisdom and skill that allow us to bring them together. Then life tastes good, because we are in tune with the glory of our being. Because we are free from self-interest, we have authentic presence and confidence—a field of power that radiates. We develop an aura that makes us seem bigger and more beautiful to others. This attracts the blessing energy of drala.

To rule our world, we need to make these Shambhala teachings our own experience. Sometimes people write down bits of wisdom and post them on the refrigerator. That is a very sweet gesture, but if we do not take those words and incorporate them into our lives, they are only decoration. Even if we are deeply inspired by this book, if we don't follow the instructions for contemplating the strategies of rulership, our inspiration will be short-lived. When we try to apply them to our lives, we will become disheartened, because it will feel nearly impossible. We have to internalize them. That's the power of contemplation. It's like kneading water into dough—we have to keep working it in. Otherwise we might hear the truth, but most likely it won't stick. We'll just go back to how we were doing things before. Learning to rule our world is not easy, but it helps that every enlightened person has undergone the process of studying these principles and working them into their lives. If we also contemplate these principles in formal sitting practice and throughout our day, everyone will definitely benefit.

If enough of us learn how to rule our world, we will eventually be able to rule our planet in a way that reflects our innate sanity as truly human beings. When we create the right conditions for success, windhorse doesn't just gallop, it flies. The effect may be gradual, but even a ten percent effort by a small number of us could enlighten the world sooner than we think. Virtue has the power of a hundred thousand suns. If even some of us turn our minds toward virtue just ten percent of the time, we will soon be living on a planet illuminated by the power of several billion suns. The Shambhala teachings tell us that when that light shines, the happiness of all sentient beings will be accomplished, and the new golden age will dawn.

A few years ago, my friend Greg told me that his brother was going on an expedition to climb Mount Everest. He asked me if there were something I would like him to take. I gave him the flag of Shambhala. The Shambhala flag has a white background representing basic goodness. It has a yellow circle representing the Great Eastern Sun, the inherent wisdom of all beings. It has four stripes, of orange, white, red, and blue, representing the four kinds of confidence—the tiger, the lion, the garuda, and the dragon. These represent the contentment, joy, equanimity, and wisdom it takes to rule our world.

In Tibet, when you reach the top of a mountain you unfurl a flag, the idea being that the wind will carry the confidence of windhorse and basic goodness in all directions. At
the same time, you shout the warriors' cry, "LHA GYAL
LO"—"Heaven is victorious."

As Greg's brother approached the top of the mountain,
the weather changed and he was unable to continue. One of
the Sherpas took the flag and carried it to the top. A lull
in the wind allowed him to unfurl the full-size flag and raise
it. The profound, brilliant, just, powerful, all-victorious way
of the ruler has been taught and practiced in Tibet and Central Asia for centuries. Now a huge nylon flag from the West
is radiating the confidence of windhorse from the rooftop of
the world. May its blessing inspire each of us to rule our
world, bringing the golden age of peace, true wealth, freedom, and happiness to all.

By this merit, may all attain omniscience
May it defeat the enemy, wrongdoing
From the stormy waves of birth, old age, sickness, and death
From the ocean of samsara, may I free all beings.

By the confidence of the Golden Sun of the Great East
May the lotus garden of the Rigdens' wisdom bloom
May the dark ignorance of sentient beings be dispelled
May all beings enjoy profound, brilliant glory.

Appendix A

The Posture of Meditation

1. The spine is upright, with its natural curves.

2. The hands are resting on the thighs.

3. The arms and shoulders are relaxed.

4. The back of the neck is relaxed, which allows the chin to come down.

5. The gaze is downward; the eyelids are half shut.

6. The face and jaw are natural and relaxed.

7. If you're sitting on a cushion, keep your ankles loosely crossed. If you're sitting on a chair, keep both feet firmly on the floor.

Appendix B

Guidelines for Breathing Meditation

1. Take the posture of meditation.

2. Make a clear and precise beginning to your practice: "Now I will begin to work with my mind and develop peace."

3. Place your mind on the breath. Stay with its flow, which soothes the mind, allows for steadiness and relaxation, and reduces discursiveness. This is ordinary breathing; nothing is exaggerated. If you're having a hard time staying with the breath, you can count the in- and out-cycles: in and then out—one; in and then out—two. If you use this method, count seven or twenty-one breaths and then start over. If you become distracted and lose count, start over again at one. Once you are more focused, you can drop the counting.

4. When you notice that you're caught up in thinking, acknowledge it. Label it "thinking," if you wish. Recognizing and acknowledging the thought allows it to dissipate as you return the placement of your mind to the breath: "Now I am placing my mind on the breath."

5. Talking about your meditation practice with someone else and being part of a community of fellow meditators can be a tremendous support. See the Resources section for help in locating a meditation instructor. Shambhala Centers offer a program based on the detailed instruction presented in my first book, *Turning the Mind into an Ally*.

Appendix C

Guidelines for
Contemplative Meditation

1. Calm the mind by resting on the breathing.

2. When you feel ready, bring up a certain thought or intention in the form of words.

3. Use these words as the object of meditation, continually returning to them as distractions arise.

4. In order to help rouse the heartfelt experience of their meaning, think about the words. Bring ideas and images to mind to inspire the meaning.

5. As the meaning of the words begins to penetrate the heart, let the words drop away, and rest in that.

6. Conclude your session and arise from your meditation with the meaning in your heart. "Meaning" is direct experience, free from words.

7. Now enter the world aspiring to conduct yourself
   with the view of your contemplation. For example,
   if you have been contemplating the preciousness
   of human birth, your view will be one of
   appreciation.

Resources

For information regarding meditation instruction or inquiries about a practice center near you, please contact one of the following:

Shambhala
1084 Tower Road
Halifax, NS
Canada B3H 2Y5
phone: (902) 425-4275, ext. 10
fax: (902) 423-2750

Web site: www.shambhala.org. This Web site contains information about the more than 100 centers affiliated with Shambhala worldwide.

Shambhala Europe
Kartäuserwall 20
50678 Cologne
Germany

phone: 49 (0) 221 310 2401
Web site: www.shambhala-europe.org
e-mail: info@shambhala-europe.org

Karmê Chöling
369 Patneaude Lane
Barnet, VT 05821
phone: (802) 633-2384
fax: (802) 633-3012
e-mail: karmecholing@shambhala.org

Shambhala Mountain Center
4921 Country Road 68C
Red Feather Lakes, CO 80545
phone: (970) 881-2184
fax: (970) 881-2909
e-mail: info@shambhalamountain.org

Sky Lake Lodge
P.O. Box 408
Rosendale, NY 12472
phone: (845) 658-8556
e-mail: skylake@shambhala.org

Dechen Chöling
Mas Marvent
87700 St Yrieix sous Aixe
France
phone: 33 (0) 55-03-55-52

fax: 33 (0) 55-03-91-74
e-mail: dechen-choling@shambhala.org

Dorje Denma Ling
2280 Balmoral Road
Tatamagouche, NS
Canada B0K 1V0
phone: (902) 657-9085
e-mail: denma@shambhala.org

Gampo Abbey
Pleasant Bay, NS
Canada B0E 2P0
phone: (902) 224-2752
e-mail: gampo@shambhala.org

Meditation cushions and other supplies are available through:

Samadhi Cushions
30 Church Street
Barnet, VT 05821
phone: (800) 331-7751
Web site: www.samadhistore.com
e-mail: info@samadhicushions.com

Drala Books and Gifts
1567 Grafton St.
Halifax, NS

Canada B3J 2C3
phone: (877) 422-2504
Web site: www.drala.ca
e-mail: drala@eastlink.ca

Naropa University is the only accredited Buddhist-inspired university in North America. For more information, contact:

Naropa University
2130 Arapahoe Avenue
Boulder, CO 80302
phone: (800) 772-6951
Web site: www.naropa.edu

Information about Sakyong Mipham Rinpoche, including his teaching schedule and a gallery of photographs, is available at his Web site: www.mipham.com.

Audio and videotape recordings of talks and seminars by Sakyong Mipham Rinpoche are available from:

Kalapa Recordings
1678 Barrington Street, 2nd floor
Halifax, NS
Canada B3J 2A2
phone: (902) 421-1550
fax: (902) 423-2750
Web site: www.shambhalashop.com
e-mail: shop@shambhala.org

The *Shambhala Sun* is a bimonthly Buddhist magazine founded by the late Chögyam Trungpa Rinpoche and now directed by Sakyong Mipham Rinpoche. For a subscription or sample copy, contact:

Shambhala Sun
P.O. Box 3377
Champlain, NY 12919-9871
phone: (877) 786-1950
Web site: www.shambhalasun.com

Buddhadharma: The Practitioner's Quarterly is an in-depth, practice-oriented journal offering teachings from all Buddhist traditions. For a subscription or sample copy, contact:

Buddhadharma
P.O. Box 3377
Champlain, NY 12919-9871
phone: (877) 786-1950
Web site: www.thebuddhadharma.com

Glossary

basic goodness The unconditional purity and confidence
  of all.

bodhichitta The wish-fulfilling jewel of wisdom, compassion,
  and courage. The mind of enlightenment.

dharma In Buddhism, the truth about the way things are; also,
  teachings that express that truth.

drala Literally, "above the enemy." The blessing energy that
  arises when we overcome our own aggression.

drip Contamination and obscuration that arise from negative
  emotions and self-centeredness.

karma Confused action based on a mistaken belief in "me" and
  "other." The intentional activity of body, speech, and
  mind created by the interdependency of causes and
  conditions.

klesha Confused emotion rooted in ignorance.

lungta Windhorse, the innate ability to attain success that
  occurs from acting virtuously.

nyingje Literally, "noble heart." Compassion, the wish for suffering to cease in all beings.

payu Discernment.

prajna "Best knowledge," incisive insight. In Tibetan iconography, it is symbolized by a sword.

Rigden "Possessor of the family." Embodiment of basic goodness. The name given to the twenty-five enlightened rulers of the legendary kingdom of Shambhala.

Rinpoche A Tibetan honorific meaning "precious jewel."

sakyong "Earth-protector." Title of the king of Shambhala. The queen is called sakyong wangmo, "earth-protector powerful lady." Representatives of the Rigdens, the king and queen of Shambhala are benevolent rulers who join heaven and earth to bring about an enlightened world.

samsara "Circular." An endless cycle of suffering and discontent, arising out of ignorance.

tashi tendrel Auspicious coincidence.

wangthang "Field of power." A quality of genuine presence that grows from our intimacy with virtue.

windhorse See **lungta**.

ziji Brilliant confidence.

Acknowledgments

I would like to offer respect and love to the Druk Sakyong, Chögyam Trungpa Rinpoche, my father, who personally manifested all the qualities described in this book and was courageous enough to utter the words "basic goodness," "compassion," and "wisdom," enabling many to raise their gaze and see the Great Eastern Sun, thus bringing true joy to people's lives; and to my mother, Lady Kunchok Palden, for her loving support and interest in everything I do.

For their wisdom and friendship, my thanks to Khenpo Namdrol, Lama Pegyal, Lama Chönam, and Khenpo Gawang. I am especially grateful to Khenpo Gawang for his enthusiasm, support, and incredible insight.

I would like to express my love and admiration for Amy Hertz of Morgan Road Books for supporting myself and many others in bringing wisdom to the world. Thanks also to Marc Haeringer of Morgan Road Books for his precision and dedication, and to my agent, Reid Boates, for our auspicious meeting and subsequent friendship.

For their generosity, I wish to thank Mark Butler, Jane

Carpenter Cohn, Jeff Cohn, Cassell Gross, Karl Gross, James Hoagland, Sharon Hoagland, Jeff Waltcher and the staff of Shambhala Mountain Center, and Ben Webster.

For their support and friendship in all kinds of ways, thanks to Richard Reoch, David Brown, Dinah Brown, Allya Canepa, Diana Church, Michael Fraund, Matt Harris, Kevin Hoagland, Adam Lobel, Ian McLaughlin, Ben Medrano, Peter Meinig, Jon Pratt, Justin Robbins, Marvin Robinson, John Rockwell, Stephan Rother, David Sell, John Sell, Josh Silberstein, Nick Trautz, Michael Weiss, and Denise Wuensch.

Most of all, I want to thank Emily Hilburn Sell for giving over her life so that this book could happen. It was truly a joy to work with her so that these precious teachings could be brought to the world.

ABOUT THE AUTHOR

Born in India in 1962, Sakyong Mipham Rinpoche is the spiritual and family successor of his father, Vidyadhara the Venerable Chögyam Trungpa Rinpoche. He is the living holder of the Shambhala Buddhist tradition, a lineage that descends through his family, the Mukpo clan. This tradition emphasizes the basic goodness of all beings and teaches the art of courageous warriorship based on wisdom and compassion. The Sakyong is an incarnation of Mipham Jamyang Gyatso (1846–1912), one of the most revered meditation masters and scholars of Tibet. Educated in Buddhist meditation, philosophy, and ritual as well as calligraphy, poetry, and archery, Sakyong Mipham Rinpoche was raised in both Eastern and Western traditions. He holds the Nyingma and Kagyü lineages of Tibetan Buddhism. He teaches throughout the world.

For more information see Sakyong Mipham's Web site at www.mipham.com.